Soft Skills:
Essential Key for Corporate Threshold

Soft Skills
Essential Key for Corporate Threshold

Deepika Nelson

 **BS Publications**
A unit of **BSP Books Pvt., Ltd.**
4-4-309/316, Giriraj Lane,
Sultan Bazar, Hyderabad - 500 095

Soft Skills: Essential Key for Corporate Threshold by Deepika Nelson

Copyright © 2020, *by Publisher*

All rights reserved. No part of this book or parts thereof may be reproduced, stored in a retrieval system or transmitted in any language or by any means, electronic, mechanical, photocopying, recording or otherwise without the prior written permission of the publishers.

Published by :

BSP BS Publications
A unit of **BSP Books Pvt., Ltd.**

4-4-309/316, Giriraj Lane, Sultan Bazar,
Hyderabad - 500 095
Phone : 040 - 23445600, 23445688
e-mail : info@bspbooks.net
website: www.bspbooks.net

ISBN : 978-93-90211-24-1

Preface

"Give us the tools, we will finish the job", said Winston Churchill at a crucial period of World War II. See how effective the message is America acted on the appeal. That is a masterly way of communication.

Substance and *style* are two facets of communication. What we say and how we say are two keys to success. *Just having technical knowledge and no communication knowledge and skill is like having one leg amputated.* Knowing what and how to communicate at an appropriate time is a skill as well as a major step towards becoming an effective communicator. People in organizations typically spend over 75% of their time in interpersonal situation; thus it is no surprise to find that at the root of a large number of organizational problems is poor communication. Effective communication is an essential component of organizational success whether it is at the interpersonal, intergroup, intragroup, organizational, or external levels.

This book will help readers refine their existing communications skills, while learning how to communicate effectively via various mediums, including the Internet and other technologies. Secondly, in the present-day context, it is essential for every institution, particularly the engineering colleges, to deal with the aspects of fostering the students with technical inputs for their academic excellence and nurturing their communication and soft skills to increase their employability potential. Through this book an effort is made by the author to fill the void between the corporate expectations and the actual skill level of the students.

Addressing a wide range of interests of students from a variety of majors, this book ***Soft Skills: Essential Key for Corporate Threshold*** has an expanded emphasis on the realities of the workplace. This is reflected in a new feature, as well as expanded content throughout focusing on what goes on in the workplace day-to-day.

Acknowledgement

I am highly grateful to Dr. K. Lakshminarayana, Director of Indur Institute of Technology, for giving me this opportunity to share my thoughts in the form of words for those who are standing on the threshold of the corporate world and striving hard to get success. At his suggestion, I designed a Key for the engineering and technical students. He has been a source of constant inspiration to me in writing this book.

I thank my department staff members for taking pains to go through the manuscript and suggest necessary changes.

I am grateful to my family members and friends who shared their corporate experiences and motivated me to inscribe and show a path for those who are right on the corporate threshold.

- Author

Key Skills and Learning Opportunities

Dear Students,

We extend a warm welcome to the academic world of Engineering and Technology.

You are on the threshold of an educational journey spanning four years of challenge and opportunity.

This is an excellent opportunity to discover your full potential, a voyage to self discovery to become a full fledged engineer.

We hope you will stand to meet the Expectation.

With Best Wishes.

We have the 'Right Attitude, caliber, competence and confidence.

Effective communication is a vital skill for everyone in business today. Great communicators have distinct advantage in building influence and jumpstarting their careers. This practical guide offers readers a clear and comprehensive overview on how to communicate effectively for every business situations.

> *Let's go forth together,*
> *Protecting each other,*
> *Together in the taste of being,*
> *Together in the trial of knowing*
> *May what is and what is known shine forth*
> *In this immense journey through light*
> *May we know no hate, only*
> *Peace and Peace and Peace*
> *Always...................*

Let's enter the world of corporate

Precision of communication is important, more important than ever, in our era of hair-trigger balances, when a false or misunderstood word may create as much disaster as a sudden thoughtless act.

James Thurber

India Vision 2020

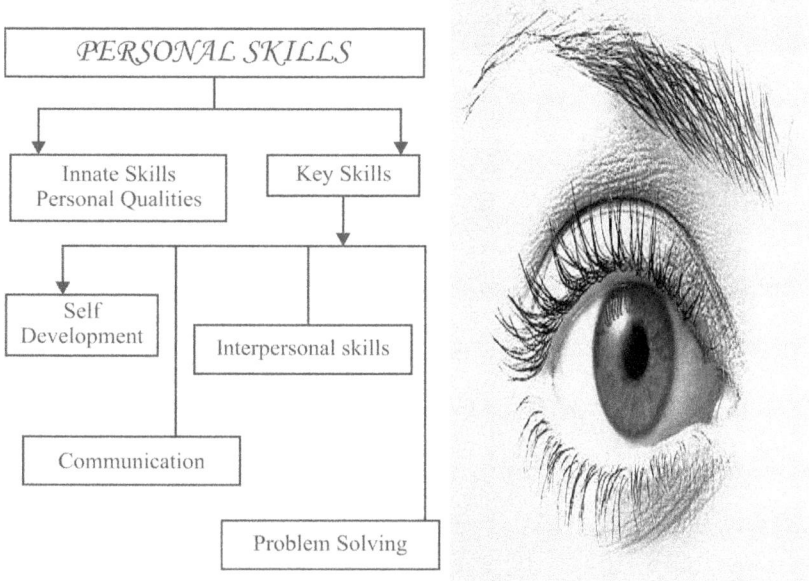

"*The reason why many do not perform to their potential is that they do not know what qualities make up their potential, what is required to perform and how to minimize the gap*"

Contents

Preface .... *(v)*
Acknowledgement .... *(vii)*

Chapter 1
    Introduction 1

Chapter 2
    Self Developmental Skills 3
        Ability to work under pressure 5
        Creative Thinking 5
        Memory 11
        Time Management 17

Chapter 3
    Communication Skill 28
        Reading 30
        Writing 37
        Listening 50
        Speaking 68
        Conference 70
        Presentation 72
        Objectives of Communication 75
        Delivery 84
        Interviewing 91
        Group Discussion 120
        Role Play 134
        Elocution 134
        Impromptu 137

Chapter 4

Interpersonal Skills **139**
    Leadership 139
    Teamwork 140
    Networking 140
    Body Language 141

Chapter 5

Resume Writing **145**
    How to write Resume 153
    Elements of a Resume 154
    Resume Format 159

Chapter 6

Cover Letter **167**
    Cover letter Format 170

Chapter 7

Problem Solving Skills **172**
    Technical Report & Proposal Writing 173

Chapter 8

Correspondence Techniques **196**
    Business Letters 197
    Organizing Your Writing –Memo Writing 203
    Effective E-mail Writing 205

Bibliography 212

CHAPTER - 1

INTRODUCTION

Innate skills are the characteristics we often think of as personality traits.

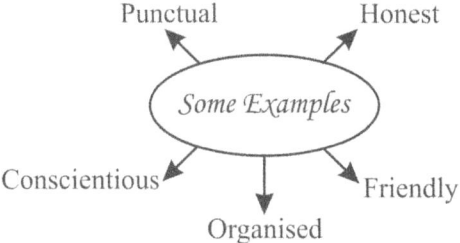

They are the skills we use in all areas of our life.

Key Skills: You May ask What ???????.

People use different synonyms including personal, transferable, generic, key, common and employable skills.

What are these Skills / Competencies / Capabilities or learning outcomes?

"All Words describe the same"

The question is, not what you know, but what you can do with what you know. u know.

Key skills described in this booklet are :

1. *Self Development :*
   Ability to work under Pressure, Goal Setting, creative thinking, memory, study and time management.

2. *Communication :*

   Reading, Writing, Listening, Speaking Verbal / Non verbal, conference presentation, Objectives Of Communication, Delivery interviewing, G D, Role Play Impromto.

3. *Interpersonal Skills :*

   Developing Team effectiveness, group discussion, acting assertively, negotiating and interviewing. Body language

4. *Problem solving skills :*

   Reports planning and research, Identifying and defining problems, Searching for retrieving Information, Generating and Evaluating Ideas, Analyzing, appraising risk and decision making, Technical Report writing

5. *Correspondence Technique :*

   Business letters, Parts Of Business Letters, Format Of Business Letters, Memo writing, Effective E-mail Writing.

CHAPTER - 2

Self Development Skills

To set Your Goal
Succeeding in today's world demands that you read, listen, speak, and write effectively. Goal setting is a standard technique used by top-level athletes, successful business-people and achievers in all fields. It gives you long-term vision and short-term motivation. It focuses your acquisition of knowledge and helps you to organize your resources.

Concentrate on results, not on being busy
Many people spend their days in a frenzy of activity, but achieve very little because they are not concentrating on the right things. This is neatly summed up in the Pareto Principle, or the '80:20 Rule'. This argues that typically 80% of unfocussed effort generates only 20% of results. The remaining 80% of results are achieved with only 20% of the effort. While the ratio is not always 80:20, this broad pattern of a small proportion of activity generating non-scalar returns recurs so frequently as to be the norm in many areas.

You should develop a vision for yourself. Where will you be five years from now?

SMART move comes only by motivation.

> S - SPECIFIC,
> M - MEASURABLE,
> A - ACTION ORIENTED,
> R - REALISTIC,
> T - TIME MANAGEMENT

Adopting the "Continuous Learning" Perspective: Seeing Every Conversation as an Opportunity to Grow --Making Better Communication an Important Part of Everyday Living.

To give a broad, balanced coverage of all important areas in your life, try to set goals in some or all of the following categories:

- *Artistic :*

  Do you want to achieve any artistic goals? If so, what?

- *Attitude :*

  Is any part of your mindset holding you back? Is there any part of the way that you behave that upsets you? If so, set a goal to improve your behavior or find a solution to the problem.

- *Career :*

  What level do you want to reach in your career?

- *Education :*

  Is there any knowledge you want to acquire in particular? What information and skills will you need to achieve other goals?

- *Family :*

  Do you want to be a parent? If so, how are you going to be a good parent? How do you want to be seen by a partner or by members of your extended family?

- *Financial :*

  How much do you want to earn by what stage?

- *Physical :*

  Are there any athletic goals you want to achieve, or do you want good health deep into old age? What steps are you going to take to achieve this?

- *Pleasure :*

  How do you want to enjoy yourself? - you should ensure that some of your life is for you!

- *Public Service :*

  Do you want to make the world a better place by your existence? If so, how?

Ability to work under Pressure

Working at your optimum efficiency during the normal course of work, you are more likely to be able to respond appropriately and handle pressure in emergency situations. You can work at your optimum efficiency by planning for work.

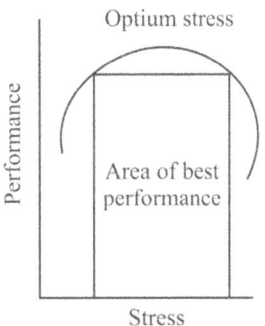

Appearing for a competitive examination usually one has to go to a special time and work in conditions which aren't familiar. You're in a place with lots of other people, not in the safety of your own room where you usually work. There are invigilators there to make sure that nobody cheats, this puts pressure on you. But working under pressure is an art an important skill too. Anxiety about results creates pressure. You will be required to meet deadlines and work for long hours. Short term pressures in modernization can actually improve your performance.

Creative Thinking

We can do Project A or Project B. Do you want more time or more money? You can have a great marriage and average career or average marriage and great career. I've got yellow or red, which do you want?

Win or lose. Yes or no. The world is black or white. You can have this or that. Which do you prefer? We must choose.

All of the statements and questions above are examples of *either/or* thinking. All of them pre-suppose that we live in a world bounded by the choice of either this or that one or the other.

These statements are founded on the belief that our world is limited. All of these choices are fundamentally rooted in the "lack mentality."

I believe there is another option. This option will give you more choices; it will improve your outlook and attitude and the quality of your life (It also may contribute greatly to improving your standard of living).

This second approach expands our thinking and is based on a belief that there is plenty in the world for everyone – plenty of time, opportunities, money, resources, people, fun, experiences. I call it "both/and" thinking. This mindset is rooted in the "abundance mentality."

Keys to both/and thinking

There are four keys to developing and using "both/and" thinking. Recognize that at the start (and in the end) utilizing this mental approach is a habit – a habit that you can nurture and develop.

Believe in abundance

It starts with a belief that more is available to us – in terms of possibilities, resources, opportunities and approaches. When we believe this is true we will begin our search for more options.

Operate on faith

Even if your belief in abundance isn't yet strong, operate on faith. Have faith that it is true, even if you can't see it or feel it yet.

Ask the question

To see the options you have to ask the question, "why not both?" Or variations like, "How can we do both?" "What would we have to modify or adjust to achieve both of these?" "Why do we have to choose?" You get the idea.

Consider the possibilities

Once you have asked the question, be open to the options and you'll be amazed at how many will show up for you.

> *"Don't be confused! Encouraging creativity is not about having meetings in hotels, nor is it about having an annual brainstorming session. It's about building a culture that encourages ideas and innovation."*
>
> *- by Andy Hanselman*

Quiz: Are You Creative?

Worried you may not be creative or you may not be creative enough? This quiz will help you find out just how creative you are.

Take a piece of paper and number it from one to seven. For each question, write down the corresponding letter of your answer.

1. *When you come across a rose, you immediately :*
    A. Smell it.
    B. Quote every rose poem you can remember.
    C. Write your own poem.
    D. Sketch the rose.
    E. Step on the rose.

Self Development Skills

2. *One of your dreams in life is to :*
   A. Write a novel.
   B. Become a painter.
   C. Travel the world.
   D. Climb all the famous mountains.
   E. Just once, get everything done on your to-do list.

3. *Your desk :*
   A. You have trouble finding as it's buried under everything including the kitchen sink.
   B. Resembles a natural disaster.
   C. Is a bit of a mess, but you know where everything is.
   D. Is basically neat – you use the stacking method
   E. Is in perfect order – everything in its place.

4. *The person you admire most is:*
   A. Einstein.
   B. Walt Disney.
   C. Your mother.
   D. Jane Austin.
   E. Anyone who can get everything crossed off his or her to-do list.

5. *You consider yourself :*
   A. Extremely creative.
   B. Creative.
   C. Somewhat creative.
   D. A little creative.
   E. About as creative as a turnip (come to think about it, turnips may be more crative then you are).

6. *You get new ideas :*
   A. All the time.
   B. Several times a week.
   C. Several times a month.
   D. Once or twice a month.
   E. You dimly recall getting a new idea when Clinton was in office. Or maybe it was the first Bush.

7. *You dream in :*
   A. Color.
   B. Black and white.
   C. Both black and white and color.
   D. You can't remember now.
   E. Nothing. You don't dream.

Scoring

Throw out all your answers except for number five -- "You consider yourself:". If you answered:
   A. Extremely creative -- Then you're extremely creative.
   B. Creative -- Then you're creative.
   C. Somewhat creative -- Then you're somewhat creative.
   D. A little creative -- Then you're a little creative.
   E. About as creative as a turnip -- Then you're about as creative as a turnip.

> *Case Study :* A couple of studies illustrate this.
>
> A big company wanted to increase creativity in its employees. So it hired a group of consultants to come in. The consultants started by thoroughly testing all of the employees.
>
> They discovered the only difference between the employees who were creative and those who weren't was this: Creative people believed they were creative and less creative people believed they weren't.
>
> Even more telling was what happened to the group that wasn't creative. The consultants focused on helping them nurture their creativity. At the end, those employees were actually more creative than the ones who had initially considered themselves creative.
>
> And that means you too can become more creative. In fact, how creative you become is entirely in your own hands.

We are entering an age where intangible assets like expertise, intelligence, speed, agility, imagination, maneuverability, networks, passion, responsiveness and innovation – all facets of knowledge – become more important than tangibles of traditional balance sheet perspectives. Todays Emerging knowledge is 'BRAIN BASED.'

Interpersonal Creativity : **Develop creative solutions to the problems you face**

The first is technical creativity, where people create new theories, technologies or ideas. This is the type of creativity we discuss here. The second is artistic creativity, which is more born of skill, technique and self-expression.

Approaches to Creativity

There are two main strands to technical creativity: programmed thinking and lateral thinking. Programmed thinking relies on logical or structured ways of creating a new product or service.

Programmed Thinking & Lateral Thinking

Lateral thinking recognizes that our brains are pattern recognition systems, and that they do not function like computers. It takes years of training before we learn to do simple arithmetic - something that computers do very easily. On the other hand, we can instantly recognize patterns such as faces, language, and handwriting. The only computers that begin to be able to do these things do it by modeling the way that human brain cells work.

The benefit of good pattern recognition is that we can recognize objects and situations very quickly. Imagine how much time would be wasted if you had to do a full analysis every time you came across a cylindrical canister of effervescent fluid. Most people would just open their can of fizzy drink. Without pattern recognition we would starve or be eaten. We could not cross the road safely.

Unfortunately, we get stuck in our patterns. We tend to think within them. Solutions we develop are based on previous solutions to similar problems. Normally it does not occur to us to use solutions belonging to other patterns.

We use lateral thinking techniques to break out of this patterned way of thinking.

Lateral thinking techniques help us to come up with startling, brilliant and original solutions to problems and opportunities.

It is important to point out that each type of approach has its strength. Logical, disciplined thinking is enormously effective in making products and services better. It can, however, only go so far before all practical improvements have been carried out. Lateral thinking can generate completely new concepts and ideas, and brilliant improvements to existing systems.

In the wrong place, however, it can be sterile or unnecessarily disruptive

While studying for engineering you are introduced to systems thinking which is experimental to generate and test ideas. Creative thinking focuses on exploring ideas, generating possibilities, looking for many right answers rather than just one.

The Vital Raw material in our economy is ***knowledge.***

Tomorrow's wealth depends upon the development and exchange of knowledge. The most important foundation skill for knowledge workers in the new environment is the ability to communicate. With communication you are able to express your creativity the best.

Gone are the days when management expected workers to check their brains at the door and do only as told. As a knowledge worker, you'll be expected to use your brains in thinking critically. You'll be solving problems and making decisions.

Creative Methods
1. *Evolution :* Incremental Improvement.
2. *Synthesis :* Two or more ideas form a third one.
3. *Revolution :* To rebel with present one and generate a new one
4. *Reapplication :* To generate something new from the old.
5. *Changing Directions :* To change your focus on other points too, to get a new idea.

Characteristics of a Creative Person
Curious, seeks problems, enjoys challenge, optimistic, able to suspend judgment, comfortable with imagination, seeks problems as opportunities, sees problems as interesting, problems are emotionally acceptable, challenges assumptions, doesn't give up easily, perseveres and works hard.

People who use these techniques routinely are the highest achievers in all walks of life, from business to sport to public service. If you use these skills well, then you will be able to function effectively, even under intense pressure.

Using creativity
Creativity is sterile if action does not follow from it. Ideas must be evaluated, improved, polished and marketed before they have any value.

Memory
- Memory is the mother of imagination, reason and skill.
- It plays an important role in our daily life.
- It is a mental process of reading, recall, recognition and association of previous learning.

Types of Memory
A. Short Term

B. Long Term

College students are confronted with two kinds or types of memory work. The first and more common is general remembering or remembering the idea without using the exact words of the book or professor. General memory is called for in all subjects; however, the arts, social sciences and literature probably make the greatest use of this particular kind of remembering.

The other type of memory work is the verbatim memorizing or remembering the identical words by which something is expressed. This type of memorizing may be called for in all subjects but especially in law, dramatics, science, engineering, mathematics, and foreign language where the exact wording of formulas, rules, norms, law, lines in a play, or vocabulary must be remembered.

Other kinds of memory have their place and it is important for the student to know when to stop with the general idea and when to fix in mind the exact words, numbers, and symbols.

1. Understand thoroughly what is to be remembered and memorized. When something is understood, be it a name or a chemical chain it is almost completely learned, for anything thoroughly understood is well on the way toward being memorized. In the very process of trying to understand, to get clearly in mind a complex series of events, or chain of reasoning, the best possible process of trying to fix in mind for later use is being followed.
2. Spot what is to be memorized verbatim. It is a good plan to use a special marking symbol in text and notebook to indicate parts and

passages, rules, data, and all other elements which need to be memorized instead of just understood and remembered.
3. If verbatim memory is required, go over the material or try to repeat at odd times, as, for example, while going back and forth to school.
4. Think about what you are trying to learn. Find an interest in the material if you wish to memorize it with ease.
5. Study first the items you want to remember longest.
6. Learn complete units at one time as that is the way it will have to be recalled.
7. Over learn to make certain.
8. Analyze material and strive to intensify the impressions the material makes.
9. Fix concrete imagery whenever possible. Close your eyes and get a picture of the explanation and summary answer. Try to see it on the page. See the key words underlined.
10. Make you own applications, examples, illustrations.
11. Reduce the material to be remembered to your own self-made system or series of numbered steps.
12. Represent the idea graphically by use of pictorial or diagrammatic forms.
13. Make a list of key words most useful in explaining the idea or content of the lesson.
14. Form a variety of associations among the points you wish to remember. The richer the associations, the better memory.
15. Try making the idea clear to a friend without referring to your book or notes.
16. Actually write out examination questions on the material that you think you might get at the end of the term. Then write answers to your own questions. Since you now have the chance, consult the text or your notes to improve your answers.
17. Follow suggestions for reviewing. This is an important part of remembering.

Technique for Memory

1. *Organize :*
    - Scan the contents to get the general idea.

- Have an overview.
- Question yourself as to how the subject you are learning will be useful to you.
- Create association between the new information and what you already know.

2. *Use your body:*
   - What we hear is forgotten to the extent of 80% if we do not learn it actively. On the contrary 90% of what is learnt is remembered if we learn actively.
   - Passive learning does not usually lead to learning.
   - Boredom puts memory to sleep.
   - Do not learn in any single position but change your position. The neck and shoulder muscles must be relaxed.
   - Relaxation is a state of alertness.
   - Create pictures of what you have learnt or draw diagrams to improve your memory.
   - Recite and repeat what you have learnt.
   - Write down points

3. *Mind Mapping :*

   "Sometimes a picture really is worth a thousand words,

   as the saying goes".

   Remembering information is a skill many people, especially students, struggle with. It is not because you were born without the ability to remember. Just that no one has taught you HOW to memorize what you need for tests! Our brains evolved to code and interpret complex stimuli such as images, colors, structures, sounds, smells, tastes, touch, positions, emotions and language. We use these to make sophisticated models of the world we live in. Our memories store all of these very effectively.

   Mind mapping helps us communicate in at least three ways: to illustrate the components of complex situations; to show the outcomes of a series of actions; and to highlight otherwise unrecognized linkages. Help get your message across with a mind map, a diagram of the reasoning going on in your head.

> **Tips make your mnemonics more memorable :**
>
> - *Use positive, pleasant images. Your brain often blocks out unpleasant ones*
> - *Use vivid, colorful, sense-laden images - these are easier to remember than drab ones*
> - *Use all your senses to code information or dress up an image. Remember that your mnemonic can contain sounds, smells, tastes, touch, movements and feelings as well as pictures.*
> - *Give your image three dimensions, movement and space to make it more vivid. You can use movement either to maintain the flow of association, or to help you to remember actions.*
> - *Exaggerate the size of important parts of the image*
> - *Use humor! Funny or peculiar things are easier to remember than normal ones.*
> - *Similarly, rude rhymes are very difficult to forget!*
> - *Symbols (red traffic lights, pointing fingers, road signs, etc.) can code quite complex messages quickly and effectively*

4. *Here is how to form an acronym :*

Forming an acronym is a good strategy to use to remember information in any order that can be remembered. An acronym is a word that is formed from the first letter of each fact to be remembered. It can be a real word or a nonsense word you are able to pronounce.

- **Write the facts you need to remember.**
- **Underline the first letter of each fact. If there is more than one word in a fact, underline the first letter of only the first word in the fact.**
- **Arrange the underlined letters to form an acronym that is a real word or a nonsense word you can pronounce.**

"Telk" is an acronym that can be used to remember the following animals: tiger, lion, elephant, kangaroo. "Telk" is not a real word, but you can easily pronounce it

5. *Use your brain :*

   Concentrate on what you are reading and reduce interference from TV/Radio.

   Read Until the lesson is assimilated.

   Choose the time for learning as per your convenience.

6. *Recall It :*
   - Some- remember what they read.
   - Some- When they write.
   - Some- When they discuss or talk to others.
   - Some- When they practically do it.

Study Skills

Study skills are necessary for good performance in test and examination.

Some of the study skills are :
- Efficient concentrating, remembering.
- Making good notes.
- Organizing study times.
- Finding a convenient place/ location for study.
- Using library effectively.
- Writing examinations.
- Communicating effectively.
- Purposeful reading.

Timing of study :
- Prepare a list of targets for each week and day.
- Prepare a time table for yourself.
- Have some breaks during your study.
- How long you study is not that important but how well you study.
- Avoid long duration of study.

Managing Your Study Time

There are only so many hours in a day, a week, and a term. You cannot change the number of hours, but you can decide how to best use them. To be successful in school/college, you must carefully manage your study time. Here is a strategy for doing this.

16   Essential Key for Corporate Threshold

At the beginning of a term, prepare a Term Calendar. Update it as the term goes on. Here is what to do to prepare a Term Calendar.

Record your school assignments with their due dates and your scheduled tests.

- Record your planned school activities.
- Record your planned school activities.
- Record your known out-of-school activities.

Each Sunday before a school week, prepare a Weekly Schedule. Update it as the week goes on. Here is what to do to prepare a Weekly Schedule.

- Record your daily classes.
- Enter things to be done for the coming week from your Term Calendar.
- Review your class notes from the previous week to see if you need to add any school activities.

- Add any out-of-school activities in which you will be involved during the week.
- Be sure to include times for completing assignments, working on projects, and studying for tests. These times may be during the school day, right after school, evenings, and weekends. Each evening before a school day, prepare a Daily Organizer for the next day. Place a v next to each thing to do as you accomplish it. Here is what to do to prepare a Daily Organizer.
- Enter the things to do for the coming day from your Weekly Schedule.
- Enter the things that still need to be accomplished from your Daily Organizer from the previous day.

Review your class notes for the day just completed to see if you need to add any school activities.

Add any out-of-school activities in which you will be involved the next day.

Your Weekly Schedule should have more detail than your Term Calendar. Your Daily Organizer should have more detail than your Weekly Schedule. Using a Term Calendar, a Weekly Schedule, and a Daily Organizer will help you make the best use of your time.

Preparing To Study

1. *Is my Study Place available to me whenever I need it?*

   Your Study Place does you little good if you cannot use it when you need it. If you are using a Study Place that you must share with others for any reason, work out a schedule so that you know when you can use it.

2. *Is my Study Place free from interruptions?*

   It is important to have uninterrupted study time. You may have to hang a DO NOT DISTURB sign on the door or take the phone off the hook.

3. *Is my Study Place free from distractions?*

   Research shows that most students study best in a quiet environment. If you find that playing a stereo or TV improves your mood, keep the volume low.

4. *Does my Study Place contain all the study materials I need?*

   Be sure your Study Place includes reference sources and supplies such as pens and pencils, paper, ruler, calculator, and whatever else you might need. If you use a computer for your work, it should be in your Study Place .

Time Management

 You need to manage time effectively if you're going to be successful. All other things being held constant, better time management skills can improve your grades, help you keep stress in check, and help you be competitive in the career you undertake. The purpose of this book is to teach you how to manage your time to improve your academic and personal performance. It refers to research on academic self-regulation research and discusses time management strategies to help you adjust how you think about time, improve your awareness of how you use time, and make change for peak performance.

Time Management Quiz

Answer each of the following questions:
- Do you estimate how many hours you will need to study each week?
- Do you meet assignment deadlines?
- Do you begin working on semester long projects early in the semester?
- Do you write a daily "to do" list?
- Do you prevent social activities from interfering with your study time?
- Do you have a job that requires fewer than 10 hours a week?
- Do you set specific goals for each study period?
- Do you begin your study time with your most difficult assignment?
- Do you complete most of your studying during your most productive hours each day?
- Do you think of being a full-time student as you would a full-time job?

Activity

To begin, on a piece of paper make a list of the top five ways you waste your time.

Many times college students have not had to manage their time efficiently prior to college because they are bright and weren't really challenged in high school. The situation often changes in college because everyone who goes to college did well in high school but the full range of grades are assigned. Some students who received A's and B's in high school are now receiving C's and D's in college. Those receiving lower grades are probably no less capable than those receiving higher grades but often their study skills, including time management, are less effective.

- If you can identify with any part of the above paragraph, working on improving your time management may be beneficial to you.
- In this article, you will be given the opportunity to assess where your time goes and make some decisions about changes you would like to make to use your time more effectively.
- There is no one right way to manage your time; however, it is important to get to know yourself so you can make good decisions about how to use your time.
- We all have 168 hours in a week to use as we wish; however, some people make better use of this time than others. If you perceive that this is an area of your life that needs improvement, this article is for you.

The Time Management Cycle

Time management "systems" often fail because they are born of perfectionism and unrealistic expectations. For instance, some people don't initiate a time management approach until they're already falling behind in their work; they undertake time management as a means of catching up.

Their initial plans tend to cram in everything they have to do without appropriate regard for the time required. The unrealistic plans that emerge from "catch-up time management" amount to little more than an expression of renewed motivation for change but without the structure to support it. Those trying to follow crammed schedules often fall seriously behind their intended pace and abandon the plan altogether, resulting in continued time trouble. Some conclude somehow that these strategies of planning don't work for them. But, what is important isn't being perfect, it is making and using a plan that helps you accomplish your goals.

One of your best options for time management systems is to begin using a cyclical system early in the academic year.

Usually the system begins with the process of goal setting to establish a context for managing time.

The next phase of the system involves tracking time and developing an awareness for where you spend your time.

The third phase of the cycle is plan making, and this could include making to-do lists, weekly plans, monthly plans and longer-range plans.

The fourth phase of the system is self-monitoring your action. Self monitoring involves paying attention to how well you are working your plan, how accurately you have planned, how well you have forecasted for various events and so on. The ideas for self-monitoring come from important research on student academic self-regulation which emphasizes the importance of adaptation in student success.

The final phase of the cycle is time shifting and adjusting (i.e., changing where you spend your time to better match your intended use of time) in which you make corrections to the system before starting the cycle again at goal setting.

Taken together, these phases permit you to initialize a process of gradual, performance-based improvement in time management skill. Everybody wants the "quick fix", but the complexity of changes involved in really getting a grip on your time management process will take some time to move through. Resist the urge to cast aside strategies that don't promise instant results; like it or not, change takes time.

What are the elements of effective time management?
- Evaluate how you are using your time
- Determine your priorities
- Create a weekly schedule
- Maintain a to-do list
- Eliminate barriers to effective time management

There's something about a nice crunchy pickle, isn't there? I mean the aroma may make some people puke, but for me it's the taste and the juice forcing itself into your mouth like a divine cascade of flavor. As a wise man once said, "It's like a taste explosion in your mouth!"

Self Development Skills

Well, this article really has nothing to do with pickles, nor does it have anything to do with eating or wise men at all. In fact this article has nothing to do with anything tangible, unless you choose to follow along. Though you don't have to, I would strongly suggest it as you could have quite the nifty little craft project by the end of this piece!

The jar
Time Management theories have come and gone. I've tried many of these and most have failed because of the sheer amount of time I needed to commit to the theory in order to save some time. The return just never seemed to justify the cost, if you know what I mean.

The latest theory of Time Management I heard has actually caused me to stop and think about how I run my entire life. This kind of thing doesn't happen very often, and no I don't mean thinking, cheeky readers! The theory that was recently taught in a Leadership course I'm enduring is called the Pickle Jar Theory.

The theory
For those crafty people among you just go, get an empty pickle jar. Big pickle jar, you could fit at least three of the largest pickles you've ever imagined inside of it. For those of you who don't like pickles, I apologize, feel free to substitute the words "pancake jar" for "pickle jar" as needed.

Okay, so you've got yourself a pickle jar. Now, put some large rocks in it. Put in as many as you possibly can. Let me know when it's full. Now, I know you think it's full, but put a couple more in anyway.

Okay, you've got a full pickle jar that you can't fit anything else into, right? Now, put some pebbles in. Put as many in as you can possibly fit, and raise your hand and bark like a puppy when you feel your jar is full.

Now, take your full jar and take sand and, you guessed it, fill that jar until you can't possibly fit anymore in, and then add some water.

I am sure the significance of this little exercise hasn't escaped any of you. Each of us has many large priorities in our life, represented by the large rocks. We also have things which we enjoy doing, such as the pebbles. We have other things we have to do, like the sand. And finally, we have things that simply clutter up our lives and get in everywhere: water.

None of these are bad things. After all, we need the gamut of these objects – from large priorities to times of rest – in order to feel truly fulfilled. No Time Management theory should be without balance, and the Pickle Jar theory is all about balance. You make time for everything, and everything simply fits well where it is supposed to fit.

Me and my day
As an example of my pre-pickle day, my little to-do list looked a lot like this:

8:00:	check and respond to email
8:30:	check various community sites and respond where required
9:00:	ensure all web properties are running properly
9:15:	set priorities for the day
9:30:	go for a walk, grab some water
10:00:	do website maintenance, remove outdated content
11:00:	draft an article
11:30:	polish next article to go out

12:00:	ensure all things web-related are handled, running well and all questions are answered
12:30:	lunch
1:30:	do programming on latest large project
2:30:	write letters to clients to keep them abreast of changes in the last three days to their projects
3:30:	check with team on progress, deal with issues
4:30:	... etc., etc., etc.

Now, I may have actually accomplished a lot in this type of day; in fact, I typically did. All my websites were running properly, I'd written an article or two, I'd done actual work, I'd built client relationships, I'd ensured my team was working properly, so what could be wrong?

Well, take a look at the first five hours of my day. Between 8 am and 1 pm, all I manage to actually get done that couldn't fit into other times when my mind tends to wander (and I tend to do these things anyway) was a little bit of article writing.

This part of the day was really a supreme waste of time. I often went to lunch feeling like I was convincing myself that I had been productive. At the end of the day I always believed that a lot got done, but my lunch times always felt slightly depressing.

Beyond that, this schedule did not work if a client walked in and needed an exceptional amount of work done, if a site had crashed overnight, or if I had an email that required more than five minutes of attention. If anything unexpected happened, which we all know should actually be expected, my whole morning and often my entire day fell apart.

My new, improved day

In these post-pickle days, my schedule looks rather different. I now schedule in times when my rocks should get done and let my other priorities, the unexpected and little things I do all day, like surf the web, fill in the gaps. New schedule:

800:	figure out rocks for the day (literally, this is what it says!) and deal with emergencies
830:	article writing as appropriate
1000:	programming
1300:	client correspondence

Suddenly I have what feels like a more open day. I have more time for programming, I get things done earlier, I am more relaxed, my schedule is more fluid. It all works incredibly well.

In the post-pickle days I realized that I needed to really figure out what my big rocks were during the day and not schedule time for anything else in my daily routine. Email is not a rock: I can go a few minutes and, wonder of wonders, even a day or two without touching it.

Email is a lot like the phone in that even though we all have our phones on just in case an important call happens, when we look back on our year it is rare that we can remember more than one or two occasions where we absolutely needed to answer our phone or email at that precise instant.

The detractors
There are of course those in the audience who will never have practiced Time Management techniques in the past. They feel they are productive enough and get "enough" done. I'm glad, way to go, give yourselves a hand. Now, grab your jar again. Empty it.

Fill your jar with water until it is completely full. Now, try and add some sand. What do you mean it didn't work?

This is the essence of the Pickle (or Pancake) Jar Theory. By first ensuring that your large priorities are tackled, scheduled, and done for the day, you can then let the smaller but less important things in until you have somehow allowed time in your day for everything you needed to do, while still relaxing and having fun.

The value of water
I strongly encourage everyone to use at least one Time Management System. It empowers you to actually do instead of scurrying about without any goals in sight. Whether you choose this particular system or not, remember: eat the pickles before you empty the jar, they are so good!

Self Development Skills

> **May This Encourage You, Always**
>
> Don't spend major time with minor people.
>
> If there are people in your life who continually disappoint you, break promises, stomp on your dreams, are too judgmental, have different values and don't have your back during difficult times...that is not friendship.
>
> To have a friend, be a friend.
>
> Sometimes in life as you grow, your friends will either grow or go. Surround yourself with people who reflect values, goals interests and lifestyles.
>
> When I think of any of my successes, I am thankful to God from whom all blessings flow, and to my family and friends who enrich my life.
>
> Over the years my phone book has changed because I changed, for the better.
>
> At first, you think you're going to be alone, but after awhile, new people show up in your life that make it so much sweeter and easier to endure.
>
> Remember what your elders used to say,
>
> *"Birds of a feather flock together.*
> *If you're an eagle, don't hang around chickens:*
> *Chickens can't fly!"*

The Time management Tools:
- Finding out how much your time is worth.
- Making sure you concentrate on the right things.
- Checking how you really spend your time.
- Tackling the right tasks first.
- Deciding what are your personal priorities.

Explain the need for time management

There is a limited amount of time in each day.
    60 minutes in an hour
    24 hours in a day

26   Essential Key for Corporate Threshold

1440 minutes a day
7 days a week
168 hours a week
52 weeks a year

By using Time Management skills you can learn to:
- Determine which of the things you do are important, and which can be dropped
- Use your time in the most effective way possible
- Increase the time in which you can work
- Control the distractions that waste your time and break your flow
- Increase your effectiveness and reduce stress

Ten Myths about Time
1. *Myth :* Time can be managed.
2. *Myth :* The longer or harder you work the more you accomplish.
3. *Myth :* If you want something done right, do it yourself.
4. *Myth :* You aren't supposed to enjoy work.
5. *Myth :* We should take pride in working hard
6. *Myth :* You should try to do the most in the least amount of time.
7. *Myth :* Technology will help you do it better, faster.
8. *Myth :* Do one thing at a time.
9. *Myth :* Handle paper only once.
10. *Myth :* Get more done and you'll be happier.

Barriers to Effective Time Management

There are many barriers to effective time management, but they can be overcome. Here is a list of the most common barriers:

- Distractions
- Disorganization
- Perfectionism
- Procrastination
- Rigidity

"We all have time to either spend or waste and it is our decision what to do with it. But once passed, it is gone forever."

- *Bruce Lee*

Do you Know

People remember

10 pecent of what they read

20 percent of what they hear

30 percent of what they see

50 percent of what they see and hear

80 percent of what they say

90 percent of what they say and do

If you tell 100 people something without repetition

After 24 hours, 25 percent have forgotten it

After 48 hours, 50 percent have forgotten it

After 72 hours, 75 percent have forgotten it

After one week, 96 percent have forgotten it

CHAPTER - 3

COMMUNICATION SKILL

> **What's that??**
> **I know you believe you understand**
> **what you think I said**
> **BUT**
> **I am not sure you realise that what**
> **you heard is not what I meant**

Regardless of what business you are in – a large corporation, a small company, or even a home-based business – effective communication skills are essential for success.

Skills Graduate Recruiters seek

The purpose of communication is to get your message across to others. This is a process that involves both the sender of the message and the receiver. This process leaves room for error, with messages often misinterpreted by one or more of the parties involved. This causes unnecessary confusion and counter productivity.

In fact, a message is successful only when both the sender and the receiver perceive it in the same way.

Communication Skill

People spend nearly 70 percent of their waking hours communicating—writing, reading, speaking, listening

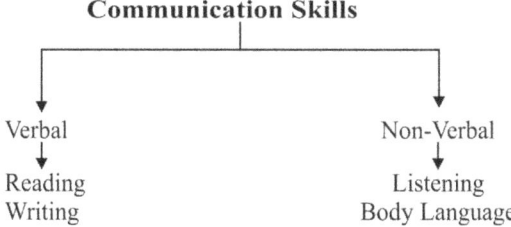

Your Words Can Make the Difference

"Praise, like gold and diamonds, owes its value to its scarcity."

Samuel Johnson

In his autobiography, My American Journey, Colin L. Powell tells of an experience when he was a colonel in Korea.

Powell had worked hard to carry out the wishes of his commanding officer, Major General "Gunfighter" Emerson. It was not an order that he agreed with. It was an attempt to impress a visiting dignitary and he felt it was a waste of time and energy for his men. Nevertheless, he dutifully accomplished the assignment.

When the ordeal was finished, Powell felt like a fraud. With his head drooping, he was visibly embarrassed. A first sergeant fell into step with him as he walked away. "That was a hoot, sir, wasn't it?"

"It was stupid," Powell blurted out. "I hate to see the troops do stupid things. And I hate to be the one responsible for it."

The sergeant was quiet for a time. "Colonel Powell, don't worry. We don't know what that was all about. But the men know you wouldn't have cooked up something that dumb on your own. They trust you. They won't hold it against you. We went along because you needed it. Relax, sir."

It was this next paragraph in General Powell's story that struck me. "In all my years in the Army, among all the citations, medals and promotions, I never appreciated any tribute more than I did the sergeant's words at that low point."

Here is one of the most admired and respected men in the world, who was deeply affected by the kind and supportive words of a subordinate. I wouldn't be surprised if that sergeant doesn't even remember saying what he did to Colin Powell that night.

No doubt there have been people in your life who have said something to you that inspired or encouraged you at an important time.

We all affect everyone else. And we rarely know when it's had an impact on someone. What we say, what we do and how we are being, can make a profound impression on others. If we're constantly looking for ways to encourage and support others, we will surely make a difference.

Who can you encourage today?

Reading

"Reading Maketh a full man"

Professionals in different fields need to read technical and business documents: reports, proposals, professional papers and magazine articles, instruction manuals etc.

Reading is the receptive skill in the written mode. It can develop independently of listening and speaking skills, but often develops along with them, especially in societies with a highly-developed literary tradition. Much like learning to drive, reading comprehension becomes so automatic that most skilled readers forget that they had to develop their reading comprehension skill. Learning reading comprehension requires a strategy where lesson plans progressively develop and reinforce reading comprehension skill.

The change in business and industrial scenario coupled with the development of advanced information technology have greatly changed the way we receive and interpret information. Reading can help build vocabulary that helps listening comprehension at the later stages, particularly Reading skills are learned bits of information that can be used to problem solve when reading or writing, enabling readers to turn writing into meaning and achieve the goals of reading independence, comprehension, and fluency.

Reading Skill

Setting a purpose is intended to give you an awareness of how to be selective in your reading of the material. In many cases a survey of the material which includes the various structures mentioned above will allow you to gain a general understanding of the material. You will identify which areas you already have some knowledge of, set approximate time limits on portions of the reading, and activate whatever knowledge they have about portions of the reading. Also, you will decide which parts to read with special emphasis. These decisions constitute the purpose a reader can use to direct himself/herself through a reading. Usually due to a fear that they will miss essential parts of the material, students are reluctant to be selective as they read. As a result, they choose to read everything as though it has equal importance to the focus of the course or to their own curiosity or needs for learning. This more thorough reading is necessary sometimes, especially when the content is something the reader has never encountered. Very frequently, however, this more thorough reading is unnecessary and costs time and may even reduce comprehension and recall for the reading.

In a sense, setting a purpose in choosing a reading process: are you intending to read to learn? to skim through to identify key concepts? scanning for something specific? The purpose or process you choose for reading changes the way you encounter the text. For example, if you were reading the newspaper you would probably not want to read it in the same way you would read portions of your text book. Likewise, if you were searching for a specific word in a dictionary, say the word "recall" you wouldn't begin by reading every word listed under every letter from A to Q in order to find it. Reading to learn, skimming, and scanning are all processes of reading which accord with a different purpose. Adjusting your reading to these various processes can make your reading both more effective and more efficient. In fact, the skills of skimming and scanning are two skills taught in courses on "speed reading" to assist in the identification of passages that should be read more thoroughly and intensively.

How To Develop Reading Skill
It turns out that our eyes can only take in information when they are stopped. What feels like continuous motion is actually move-stop-read-move-stop-read, etc. You can easily verify this by sitting face to face with a partner, holding up a book and watching their eyes as they read. The key is to minimize the number of stops by maximizing the number of words you see at each stop as shown in Figure.

The person who uses the first eye movement pattern is actually looking at every word, one at a time. The person who uses the second is still looking at every word, but in groups. The person who uses the third eye movement pattern "notices" only a few key words and does so by reading both horizontally and vertically at the same time.

"But the first reader is going to comprehend the material much better than the third!" you may be thinking. Possibly, is my reply. If the third reader actually uses all three eye movement patterns, using the slower patterns very selectively, then he has a better chance of investing his mental energies on the material of most relevance to him.

32 Essential Key for Corporate Threshold

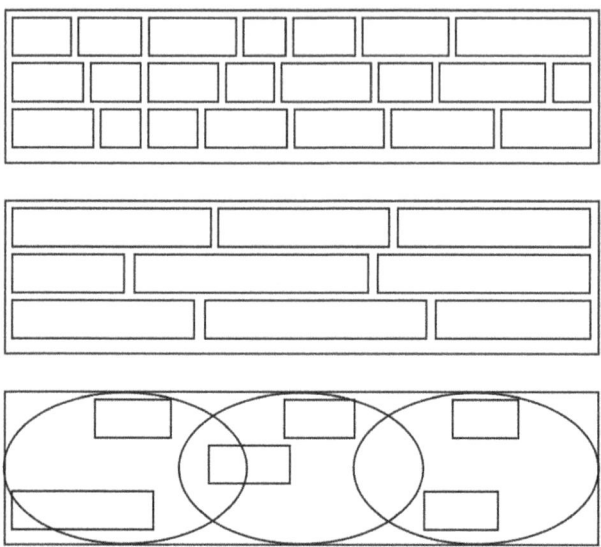

Figure. Three eye movement patterns.

"The art of becoming wise is the art of knowing what to overlook."

William James

The smart reader is one who uses the third technique to scan the entire book (overview) or chapter (preview), and then comes back and uses some combination of the first two techniques to further explore the sections of most relevance.

Getting to both the second and third levels requires a visual reading strategy. You must silence subvocalization and learn to "trust your eyes". This involves shifting your mental reading process from "see->say->understand" to just "see->understand". One way to make this leap is to build up your visualization muscle

One way to stop subvocalizing (saying words in your head while reading) is to increase the rate at which your eyes move across the page to the point where it is impossible to subvocalize. This means switching your reading strategy to a point whereby you notice gulps of words at each eye resting point. These gulps sometimes involve pulling words from multiple lines.

When I did this recently, I noticed that I was still understanding what I was reading but in a different way. I caught myself thinking: "But now I'm not really reading." In other words, part of my mind still believed that the definition of reading was to look at every word and sound it out in my mind.

Another way to look at this issue of subvocalization is that you should develop multiple reading strategies, some of which may include subvocalization and some may not. You wouldn't want a car that moves only at one speed. You want to have multiple gears (i.e., reading styles) that can be applied based on the unique demands of each situation.

The final two steps to take involve following up on your reading skills by reciting and reviewing. These are typically thought of as "study" techniques more than "reading" techniques, but I want to emphasize that reading does not take place in a vacuum. Reading, after all, is done as part of our process of learning. For this reason, recitation and reviewing are two very important facets of our reading strategy.

What is Reading Comprehension?

Reading comprehension skills separate the "passive" unskilled reader from the "active" readers. Skilled readers don't just read, they interact with the text. To help novice readers understand this concept, you might make them privy to the dialogue readers have with themselves while reading.

Skilled readers, for instance:
1. Predict what will happen next in a story using clues presented in text.
2. Create questions about the main idea, message, or plot of the text.
3. Monitor understanding of the sequence, context, or characters.
4. Clarify parts of the text which have confused them.
5. Connect the events in the text to prior knowledge or experience .

Reading Comprehension Skills

Reading comprehension is the process of understanding and constructing meaning from a piece of text. Connected text is any written material involving multiple words that forms coherent thoughts. Phrases, sentences, paragraphs, and so on, are examples of connected text that can be read with comprehension.

Lost Sheep

Lord Jesus Christ often told quite interesting stories. We call them parables. They have a hidden meaning. They teach us about God and about ourselves. A parable is an earthly story with a heavenly meaning. Listen to this parable called, "The lost sheep". Have you ever seen a flock of sheep grazing in the fields or up on the hills. Perhaps they were a few little lambs frisking around. It is a lovely sight to see the sheep and their lambs. Lord Jesus told a story of a Shepherd boy who had a flock of a hundred sheep. He was a good, kind Shepherd. One day he found that one of his sheep was missing. It had wandering off and was lost. You know sheep are foolish animals they often wander away and they can never find their way back. The Shepherd, of course, was very sad. He did not forget the lost sheep, because there were so many more. Nor did he say, "well it does not matter really. I have all these others". What do you think he did? He carefully made sure that the remaining 99 of them were safe. Then he went in search of the one that had strayed.

We do not know as to how long he searched for it nor how far he did go. At last, when he found the sheep, he neither beat it nor shouted at it. Instead, he lovingly carried it on his shoulders and went back to his place. He felt so happy that he called his neighbous to share his joy and cried that he could find the sheep. Jesus Christ himself was a good Shepherd. He loved his sheep so much that he went after the wandering sheep till he found it and rejoiced as he brought it back to the field. Are we not like poor wandering sheep, so ready to sin and so ready to go astray?

We need Lord Jesus to seek us and find us. Here it is a good prayer, "Lord the wandering sheep beholds; Bring him back into thy fold; On thy shoulders bear him home. Suffer him no more to roam". This parable teaches us that even if we stray some times, God is kind and merciful to bring us back to his fold. We may perhaps apply this parable to some situations in our own lives.

> *When You read the above story you understand your eye movement, the words followed by alphabets. You also realize that when a writer translates ideas into words and sentences, he is bound by grammar and syntax and often uses more words than required. With effective reading comes Skimming which is superficial, but is quick and efficient way of familiarizing yourself with text. Scanning is a rapid search for facts and particular ideas.*

Reading Exercise
When all the people had assembled, the king, surrounded by his court, xx1xx a signal. Then a door beneath him opened, and the accused man stepped out into the arena. Directly opposite him were two doors, exactly xx2xx and side by side. It was the duty and the privilege of the person on trial to walk directly to these xx3xx and open one of them. He xx4xx open either door he pleased; he was subject to no guidance or influence but that of impartial and incorruptible chance. If he opened the one, there came out of it a hungry tiger, the fiercest and most cruel that could be found, which xx5xx sprang upon him and tore him to pieces as a punishment for his guilt. But, if the accused person opened the other door, out of it came a xx6xx lady, and to this lady he was immediately married, as a reward of his innocence. This was the xx7xx method of administering justice. Its perfect fairness is obvious. The criminal could xx8xx know out of which door would come the lady; he opened either he pleased, without having the slightest xx9xx whether, in the next instant, he was to be devoured or married. So the accused person was instantly xx10xx if guilty, and, if innocent, he was rewarded on the spot.

Adapted from The Lady or the Tiger by Frank Stockton

A SHORT HISTORY OF WRITING -

Writing as Communication

We take it for granted that we can communicate with each other by means of the written word or in pictures, but how did this ability originate in humans? How did we first realise we could make marks that others would recognise as representations of things in our world? How did we arrive at being able to draw, and write, and eventually to leave records of our existence for others to see and understand?

Perhaps the answer lies in the present rather than the past. We might go some way towards answering this question by drawing a parallel between the development of children, and how they learn the significance of signs and symbols, and the development of early human beings in general. Without delving too deeply into the psychological aspects of human development it is interesting to note that children will learn to draw, eventually, without being taught.

Given a stick or pencil, a child will begin scribbling with it at about the age of one-and-a-half. At first there is possibly only the satisfaction of the action itself, and the visual pleasure of the marks they make, that stimulates the child to continue the actions. By about the age of three a child will be drawing clear representations of things in his/her world.

The images are not works of art but eventually the child recognises things in them and, importantly, recognises that he/she can consciously make shapes that will represent things in the world around them and be recognised by others. He or she discovers, along with speech and the many gestures we make facially and bodily, that they have another means of communicating with the world.

It is tempting to assume that early humans started out in a similar way, but that something in the perceptual nature of our species set us apart from others in realising the value of this tool as a means of communication. Chimps can make marks in the dirt with a stick but they don't write to each other or draw each other pictures.

An early example of the understanding of the power of communication is evident in the cave paintings at Lascaux and numerous other sites around the world. Some of these are over 20,000 years old and are the earliest evidence of human beings recording their presence, their actions, and their environment. The communication of information, ideas, or knowledge, to another must surely be the biggest driving force for the development of drawing, and of writing systems.

Writing

Writing is very powerful - and for this reason, it can be exploited in engineering. The power comes from its potential as an efficient and effective means of communication; the power is derived from order and clarity. Structure is used to present the information so that it is more accessible to the reader.

Are you aware that one of the most time-consuming, yet important tasks busy employees have on their to-do lists is writing? E-mail inboxes are full of messages requiring responses to be sent out to those with equally overflowing message centers. The quantity of time spent to write letters, memos, proposals, and technical reports often exceeds the quality of the resulting documents.

Professional Writing Skills helps business and technical writers resolve two of their biggest written communication challenges: how to write more effective documents following a more efficient process. Participants report that the quality of their documents increases while the quantity of time needed to write them decreases, often by 1/3.

Thus it is absolutely vital for you as a Professional Engineer to actively develop the skill of writing; not only because of the time involved in writing, but also because your project's success may depend upon it. Indeed, since so much of the communication between you and more senior management occurs in writing, your whole career may depend upon its quality.

In an industrial context, writing has two major roles:

- It clarifies - for both writer and reader
- It conveys information

Academicians and business people view writing skills as crucial, yet increasing numbers of these professionals note a steady erosion in the writing abilities of graduates.

The summary of a study published in Personnel Update states: "Writing skills ... of executives are shockingly low, indicating that schools and colleges dismally fail with at least two-thirds of the people who pass through the education pipeline coming out unable to write a simple letter."

> Writing is the major means of communication within an organisation; paper is thought to be the major product of professional engineers; some estimate that up to 30% of work-time is engaged in written communication this has nothing to do with engineering writing. No engineering report will ever get such reviews. The most significant point about engineering writing is that it is totally different from the writing most people were taught - and if you do not recognize and understand this difference, then your engineering writing will always miss the mark. However, this article outlines a methodical approach to writing which will enable anyone to produce great works of engineering literature.

In 1988, Lin Grensing reported that 79 percent of surveyed executives cited writing as one of the most neglected skills in the business world, yet one of the most important to productivity.

A 1992 survey of 402 companies reported by the Associated Press noted that executives identified writing as the most valued skill but said 80 percent of their employees at all levels need to improve. The number of workers needing improvement in writing skills was up 20 percent from results of the same survey in 1991. Results of a 1993 study by Olsten Corp., a placement agency, were almost identical: 80 percent of 443 employers surveyed said their workers needed training in writing skills.

The need for workers with writing skills will only increase. A 1991 report by the U.S. Labor Department noted that most future jobs will require writing skills

Professional writing has very little to do with the composition and literature learnt at school: the objectives are different, the audience has different needs, and the rewards in engineering can be far greater. As engineers, we write for very distinct and restricted purposes, which are best achieved through simplicity.

There are many uses for paper within an organization; some are inefficient - but the power of paper must not be ignored because of that. In relation to a project, documentation provides a means to clarify and explain on-going development, and to plan the next stages. Memoranda are a simple mechanism for suggestions, instructions, and general organization. The minutes of a meeting form a permanent and definitive record.

Writing is a central part of any design activity. Quality is improved since writing an explanation of the design, forces the designer to consider and explore it fully. For instance, the simple procedure of insisting upon written test-plans forces the designer to address the issue. Designs which work just "because they do" will fail later; designs whose operation is explained in writing may also fail, but the repair will be far quicker since the (documented) design is understood.

If you are having trouble expressing an idea, write it down; you (and possibly others) will then understand it. It may take you a long time to explain something "off the cuff", but if you have explained it first to yourself by writing it down - the reader can study your logic not just once but repeatedly, and the information is efficiently conveyed.

Structure

> While still considering the aim and the reader, the document is broken down into distinct sections which can be written (and *read*) separately. These sections are then each further decomposed into subsections (and sub-subsections) until you arrive at simple, small units of information - which are expressed as a paragraph, or a diagram.
>
> Every paragraph in your document should justify itself; it should serve a purpose, or be removed.
>
> A paragraph should convey a single idea.
>
> There should be a statement of that key idea and (possibly) some of the following:
>
> - A development of the idea
> - An explanation or analogy
> - An illustration
> - Support with evidence
> - Contextual links to reinforce the structure

Layout

The main difference between written and verbal communication is that the reader can choose and re-read the various sections, whereas the listener receives information in the sequence determined by the speaker. Layout should be used to make the structure plain, and so more effective: it acts as a guide to the reader.

Suppose you have three main points to make; do not hide them within simple text - make them obvious. Make it so that the reader's eye jumps straight to them on the page. For instance, the key to effective layout is to use:

- informative titles
- white space
- variety

Another way to make a point obvious is to *use a different font.*

Many people are intimidated by writing. Even so, there are times when writing is the best way to communicate, and often times the only way to get your message across

"Writing maketh an exact man"

When writing, be mindful of the fact that once something is in written form, it cannot be taken back. Communicating through words can be more concrete than verbal communications, with less room for error and even less room for mistakes. This presents written communicators with new challenges, including spelling, grammar, punctuation, even writing style and actual wording.

Thankfully, today's technology makes memo, letter and proposal writing much easier by providing reliable tools that check and even correct misspelled words and incorrect grammar use. Unfortunately, these tools are not fail proof and will require your support, making your knowledge in this area important.

In a recent survey of recruiters from companies with more than 50,000 employees, communication skills were cited as the single more important decisive factor in choosing managers.

The survey, conducted by the University of Pittsburgh's Katz Business School, points out that communication skills, including written and oral presentations, as well as an ability to work with others, are the main factor contributing to job success.

In spite of the increasing importance placed on communication skills, many individuals continue to struggle with this, unable to communicate their thoughts and ideas effectively – whether in verbal or written format. This inability makes it nearly impossible for them to compete effectively in the workplace, and stands in the way of career progression.

The Importance of "Style"...

People in business do not have the time to marvel at your florid turn off phrase or incessant ill iteration. They want to know what the document is about and (possibly) what it says; there is no real interest in style, except for ease of access

Some of the most basic tips to remember when writing include:

Avoid the use of slang words

- **Try not to use abbreviations (unless appropriately defined)**
- **Steer away from the use of symbols (such as ampersands (&))**
- **Clichés should be avoided, or at the very least, used with caution**
- **Brackets are used to play down words or phrases**
- **Dashes are generally used for emphasis**
- **Great care should ALWAYS be taken to spell the names of people and companies correctly**

- **Quotation marks** should be placed around any directly quoted speech or text and around titles of publications.
- **Keep sentences short**

While the above tips cover the most common mistakes made when writing letters, memos and reports, they in no way cover everything you need to know to ensure your written communications are accurate and understood

Written communication is impersonal in the sense that two communicators cannot see or hear each other and cannot provide immediate feedback. Organization relies on written communication for many reasons. It provides a permanent record, a necessity in these times of litigation and extensive government regulation. Writing up an idea instead of delivering it orally enables communicators to develop an organized, well-considered message.

Unlike the oral presentation of ideas, the written presentation of ideas is governed by some very specific rules. Each of us writes in an individual "style" which we have developed over the years. We are not trying to change that style, but merely suggesting the guidelines below. These suggestions will help you edit and criticize your own (and others) written material

1. **Proofread aloud** *everything going out.* By reading aloud, your ear will catch mistakes your eye misses.

2. **Make no assumptions.** The ideas you are presenting must be explained in full to be understood. PEOPLE READ ONLY WHAT IS ON THE PAGE.

3. **Do not lecture.** Write only what must be understood to make the proper decision or choice.

4. **Rough draft** all important letters and reports. Check them for content, sequential development of ideas, and conciseness.

5. Always put yourself in the "other person's shoes" and ask yourself, "Would I want to read this letter or report? Why? Does it say something of value and real importance to me?"

6. Many people are too busy to read carefully. Be sure your ideas are clear and easy to follow. As a general rule, the most effective manner in which to develop an idea is:

Concept è Benefit Example è Data

This method leads your reader to the conclusion you want because the conclusion is already clearly stated as the concept (hypothesis). Your examples and data are support for the conclusion.

1. Define all "terms" and eliminate vague pronouns. These two traps cause more problems in writing than any other set of conditions.

2. Grammar, punctuation, and spelling should be perfect. Use a dictionary — either a good unabridged volume or the "spelling checker" version on your computer.

3. Plan your time to allow for proofreading and correcting. When your success depends upon the quality of your letters and reports, there are no excuses for ineptitude. There is no substitute for EXCELLENCE!

Writing Skills for Technical hand

"Say all you have to say in the fewest possible words, or your reader will be sure to skip them; and in the plainest possible words or he will certainly misunderstand them."

By. John Ruskin

> The great American author Sinclair Lewis made a huge impact on writing and writers alike. His prose remains with us today as "classic" - something that will never go out of style. Once, this author was asked to give a lecture on writing to college students. He gazed around the room and stated, "Looking out at this gathering makes me want to know how many of you really and truly wish to become writers." As might be expected, every hand in the room shot up. Sinclair Lewis looked at all the raised hands, folded his notes, and put them away before saying, "If that's true, then the best advice I can give you is to go home and start writing." Nothing more, nothing less, Lewis turned and left the room. It's a statement that writers hear over and over: If you want to be a writer, you have to write."

"I hated English; that's why I became an engineer in the first place" technical people need adequate writing skills though they despise writing. Today's work cultures major emphasis is on communication writing, reading, listening and speaking

Why (Some) Techies Can't Write

- **Writing was not part of their professional education.** Techies may have struggled through branches of Engineering during the years in college, but many did not have an upper-level writing course to help them build on-the-job writing skills. Thankfully, this situation has changed. Most colleges provide an upper-level, discipline-specific Communication (writing) course.

- **Techies frequently communicate visually.** Instead of words, they use flowcharts, blueprints, satellite images, and schematics.

- **Techies tend to be "trees" people.** They're immersed in details and may have trouble seeing the "forest." Good writing requires describing the forest, then pointing out individual trees.

- Not being able to write (or not wanting to) is part of techie culture.

Why Techies *Must* Be Able To Write

- **If they can't write, they can't share what they know.** Expert Dorothy Winsor, famous for studying the communication failures that led to the Challenger disaster, puts it this way: "Effective communication generally, and effective technical writing specifically, is essential to success in engineering because it conventionalizes knowledge and makes it shareable."

- **Poor writing skills are costly.** In 2004, the National Commission on Writing estimated that remedying deficiencies in writing costs American corporations as much as $3.1 billion annually.

- **Good writing buys techies a seat at the corporate decision-making table.** When techies represent their ideas well in writing, management can understand what techies need, want, or have accomplished.

- **When techies can *write*, the rest of the world can *do*.** Ever consulted a User Manual and found that it actually *helped* you? If so, thank a techie who could write.

Writing Exercise-To Do

> Beyond the novel that inches line-by-line toward completion or the series of articles that slowly grow day-by-day, finding things to write about that keep you fresh and your ideas flowing can be difficult. Writing exercises help open our minds and prod us to experiment, which in turn sharpens our skills as writers.

Exercise 1.

Stretch your imagination and your use of words with these five writing exercises that explore description and metaphors

1. **Open up a dictionary**. Choose a word and write about it for 10 minutes, non-stop. Choose another word and do the same. Choose a third and write 10 more minutes. Although you have three different words, there may be a common thread running through them. Look for it. The day I did this, the rainy weather permeated my three pieces of random writing. If a thread is not there, try and connect these three separate pieces of writing.

2. **Make a list about something**. Choose something ordinary and make a list of things about it or related to it. Do it off the top of your head, taking just 10 minutes or so. Now read it. You will feel a rhythm to it after a few lines, and it will sound poetic. If you make a list about a kiss or love or flowers, you may have a sweet poem when you're done.

    The class I did this in listed a yard sale. Sounds dull? It was actually very interesting to hear what everyone had to say about a yard sale, the contents, the seller, the other buyers, the type of day it was and so on. A yard sale is not dull subject matter!

3. **This is one of my favorites**. I came across it as I was studying metaphors. On the left side of the page, list tangible nouns. Ocean, flood, steam shovel, cinder block, spoon. On the right side of the page, list intangible nouns. Respect, desire, hunger, flight. Now combine them in a phrase like this:

    'a of '. Examples would be 'an ocean of respect', a spoonful of desire'. Let yourself get carried away with this, and you will come up with some very powerful images

46   Essential Key for Corporate Threshold

4. **Find a picture in a magazine**. Make sure it interests you. Look this picture over carefully for just a minute and write about it for at least 10 minutes. Describe the detail, the light, the subject matter. Are there people? What are they thinking? How did they get there? Who are they? You could do the traditional 'Who What When Where Why' routine. You'll be surprised at how much you can see in a picture when you have to!

5. **Take a mediocre, horrible or fabulous piece of your writing**.

    It doesn't need to be long, just writing. Go through it and look for non-descript words, such as 'nice', 'beautiful' and 'wonderful'. List these words, and detail what they are actually supposed to be describing.

    A nice outfit - Nice means as many things as there are people! Does nice mean green or blue? Cotton or polyester? A skirt or pants? Matching or eclectic?

    A beautiful day - Some folks like rain, some love the sun. Are there clouds? Is it morning or evening? Is it a day to lounge at home or go out and socialize? What constitutes a beautiful day? Beauty? What's that?

    You can see by these examples that non-descript words rob your writing of what makes it unique - you!

Exercise 2.

1. **Can you understand the paragraph? Is it clear and well organized? Are there any mistakes in it? Let's look at the writing more closely. Did the writer use a spell check? Can you find any spelling errors?**

   Green house effect is one of the phenomena caused by industrial pollution. From the data taken by scientists, our earth has been warming up since the Industrial Revolution. Why does it happen? The factories' emissions have created smog on the atmosphere. The earth's atmosphere becomes like a green house, and the earth and everything inside of it have become like the plants in the green house. The sunlight can pass trough the ozone layer but the heat transferred by the sunlight can not escape easily from the layer of smog and is deflected to earth's surface again

   Answer: After Spell check

2. What is wrong with the words green and house? There is nothing wrong with the words themselves, but the writer is not discussing a house that happens to be green. He is referring to a special kind of building in which plants are grown, and that buiding is called a greenhouse. It is one word. A reader thinking that a green house is being discussed rather than a greenhouse would be confused. This is not a serious mistake, but fixing it will certainly improve the paragraph.

   Now let's consider the word trough in the sentence below.

   The sunlight can pass trough the ozone layer but the heat transferred by the sunlight can not escape easily from the layer of smog and is deflected to earth's surface again.

   A trough is a container or a ditch. That is not what the writer meant. What do you think the spelling here should be?

   Answer: The correct spelling of the word is through. Writing trough instead of through was probably not really a spelling error but a typing mistake or what we call a typo. The letter h was omitted. Because trough is a real word, the spell check on the computer did not catch it. We can see that it is very important to review or proofread our work very carefully because we can not depend on the computer to find and correct all of our mistakes

48   Essential Key for Corporate Threshold

3. **Now let's move on to grammar problems. There are 3 problems with articles in the paragraph. Can you find them? Look for definite articles that have been omitted or used in place of indefinite articles.**

   Greenhouse effect is one of the phenomena caused by industrial pollution. From the data taken by scientists, our earth has been warming up since the Industrial Revolution. Why does it happen? The factories' emissions have created smog on the atmosphere. The earth's atmosphere becomes like a greenhouse, and the earth and everything inside of it have become like the plants in the green house. The sunlight can pass through the ozone layer but the heat transferred by the sunlight can not escape easily from the layer of smog and is deflected to earth's surface again.

   Answer : The 2 missing articles are shown in red below.

   The greenhouse effect is one of the phenomena caused by industrial pollution. From the data taken by scientists, our earth has been warming up since the Industrial Revolution. Why does it happen? The factories' emissions have created smog on the atmosphere. The earth's atmosphere becomes like a green house, and the earth and everything inside of it have become like the plants in the greenhouse. The sunlight can pass through the ozone layer but the heat transferred by the sunlight can not escape easily from the layer of smog and is deflected to the earth's surface again.(The place in which a definite article is used instead of the indefinite article is shown.)

   The preposition from does not fit very well. A better word choice is the phrase according to. Look at the correction indicated below in red.

4. There is another preposition problem in the following sentence:

   The factories' emissions have created smog on the atmosphere.

   What word can we use instead of the preposition on?

   Answer: In

   The End:

   Now the grammar and spelling errors have been corrected and the paragraph looks quite nice.

Let's consider the structure of the whole paragraph and make sure it is clear and logical.

The greenhouse effect is a phenomenon caused by industrial pollution. According to the data taken by scientists, our earth has been warming up since the Industrial Revolution. Why does it happen? Emissions from factories have created smog in the atmosphere. The earth's atmosphere becomes like a greenhouse, and the earth and everything inside of it have become like the plants in a greenhouse. The sunlight can pass through the ozone layer but the heat transferred by the sunlight cannot escape easily from the layer of smog and is deflected to the earth's surface again.

The Art of Listening

By Terry Wildemann

Listening is an art that when done well delivers tremendous benefits. The goal of listening well is to achieve win-win communication.

Win-win communication not only fosters understanding, affirmation, validation and appreciation, but it also creates an atmosphere of trust, honor and respect.

When someone truly listens to you, don't you feel special?

Listening well is a two-way street, and to be effective communicators, we must all listen well to each other. One-way listening can be equated to driving down a one-way street the wrong way. It's dangerous, it can get you into trouble and it can be expensive, as illustrated in the following example.

Sam, a dispatcher for a national moving company in Philadelphia, gave Mike, a new driver, an assignment to go to Portsmouth to make a household goods delivery.

When Mike arrived in Portsmouth, he called Sam for further instructions. As Sam gave Mike the necessary information, Mike got a strange feeling that something wasn't quite right.

Mike asked Sam for the complete address, which was Maple Street in Portsmouth, Virginia. Well, Mike was in Portsmouth, but it was

Portsmouth, Rhode Island. Mike was ten hours away from where he was supposed to be. He had traveled north in the wrong direction.

Not only did this cost the company time and money, but also the owner of the goods was not pleased.

What caused this expensive mistake? Ineffective listening by both parties. In his haste, Mike didn't listen to all the information that Sam gave him, and Sam neglected to get accurate acknowledgment from Mike stating that he understood the instructions.

Communication Skill 51

Focus on the Caller

Listening well is a skill that requires practice. Someone who listens well easily establishes rapport with others. Good listeners attract others because they focus on the speaker completely. They have a positive energy that makes you want to be in their company. They are effective in their jobs because, by listening and asking the appropriate questions, they know exactly what needs to be done and how to do it. To be effective when interacting over the telephone, hone your verbal skills and focus completely on what the speaker is saying.

Listen closely to your intuition. The best example of this is to observe how blind people communicate. Since they do not have the gift of sight, they focus on their other gifts and develop them. Their hearing is acute, and they can read people by focusing on a person's voice attitude and the words that the person uses.

Those of us whose work depends on the telephone should do the same.

Active Listening
Whether you are an executive, manager or line employee, one of the best things you can do for yourself is to improve your listening skills. People who listen effectively are perceived as more helpful, more "in tune" and tend to exert more influence over others than those that are less effective listeners. Paradoxically, good listeners are listened to more than poor listeners. In this book, we are going to briefly discuss effective listening, and suggest an exercise you can use in the privacy of your own home to help you enhance your listening skills. Not only can you apply them at work, but in any relationship.

Good listening is crucial to effective communication and career success. Studies show, however, that only about 10% of us listen properly. Most of us don't know how to listen intelligently, systematically and purposefully.

Think about your most recent conversations at work. If you remember what you said better than what you heard, you've probably developed some bad listening habits. Instead of really listening, you let your mind wander while others were talking. You were thinking about what you were going to say before the others had finished

We often confuse hearing with listening. While hearing is a function of biology, listening is a function of intentional behavior. It is something we choose to do, and as such, we need to build skills, and practice to be effective at it.

There are two major components to effective listening, or in other words, two families of skills that need to be mastered. The first component is your ability to focus your attention on the words, body language, and meaning of the speaker. If you are unable to focus your attention on these in a sustained manner, you will have difficulty understanding the nuances of what the speaker is expressing.

Hear Whsat People are Really Saying

What does it mean to really listen?

Real listening is an active process that has three basic steps.

1. *Hearing*: Hearing just means listening enough to catch what the speaker is saying. For example, say you were listening to a report on zebras, and the speaker mentioned that no two are alike. If you can repeat the fact, then you have heard what has been said.

2. *Understanding*: The next part of listening happens when you take what you have heard and understand it in your own way. Let's go back to that report on zebras. When you hear that no two are alike, think about what that might mean. You might think, "Maybe this means that the pattern of stripes is different for each zebra."

3. *Judging*: After you are sure you understand what the speaker has said, think about whether it makes sense. Do you believe what you have heard? You might think, "How could the stripes to be different for every zebra? But then again, the fingerprints are different for every person. I think this seems believable."

Exercise 1. Developing Attention-Focusing Skills

speaking it is much easier to develop empathetic listening skills than it is to acquire focusing. Lets take a simple technique to use to practice attention focusing. Attention focusing is a mental discipline, regardless of context. All it requires is a television, or radio, and a few minutes of uninterrupted time available on a regular basis.

1. Find a television or radio program that approximates real talk. In other words, the ideal program would have some period where the speaker talks for several minutes, uninterrupted. A sermon, speech or lecture is ideal. The telecasts of parliament or government proceedings might be ideal, and since these are generally available in most areas via cable, they are also easy to find.

2. Give the speaker your full attention. listen to the words AND watch the body language. Most people will find that stray thoughts intrude quite quickly, sometimes as often as every ten or fifteen seconds. Each time your mind wanders, "grab it" and refocus on the speaker. Don't get discouraged if you must do this many times. It will get easier.

3. Once you are able to listen with full attention to the TV/radio speaker, for a period of ten minutes, you will be ready to start practicing with people in person. Time yourself, since it is easy to misjudge the time when you are trying to listen.

Think about your most recent conversations at work/college. If you remember what you said better than what you heard, you've probably developed some bad listening habits. Instead of really listening, you let your mind wander while others were talking. You were thinking about what you were going to say before the others had finished. Good listening is crucial to effective communication and career success. Studies show, however, that only about 10% of us listen properly. Most of us don't know how to listen intelligently, and systematically.

The higher the manager is on the corporate ladder, the more time He/she spends listening to others. Interestingly, most appraisal studies find that managers who are rated most efficient by subordinates invariably are good listeners. In job interviews, many candidates fail to impress managers because they listen so poorly. Recruiting managers regard good listening skills as crucial and use feedback to determine how well candidates listen.

Answering questions incorrectly, or failing to grasp an interviewer's point, will sound the death knell on job offers.

It is obvious to say that if you have poor interpersonal communications skills (which include active listening), your productivity will suffer simply because you do have the tools needed to influence, persuade and negotiate – all necessary for workplace success. Lines of communications must be open between people who rely on one another to get work done. Considering this, you must be able to listen attentively if you are to perform to expectations, avoid conflicts and misunderstandings, and to succeed - in any arena.

Challenge 1:
listen first & acknowlefdge

We were given two ears but only one mouth.

This is because God knew that listening was twice as hard as talking.

This segment is designed to help you understand the importance of improving your listening skills, and giving you the techniques to improve this vital skill.

> *The reason you don't understand me, Harry, is because I'm talkin' to you in English and you're listenin' to me in dingbat!"? - Shally*
>
> *Shally was right about finding a common language or wavelength, but it takes two to communicate— the speaker and the listener. Both need to make the effort to understand each other. According to a French proverb, "The spoken word belongs half to him that speaks and half to him who hears."*

The first skill that you can practice to be a good listener is *to act like a good listener*. We have spent a lot of our modern lives working at tuning out all of the information that is thrust at us. It therefore becomes important to change our physical body language from that of a deflector to that of a receiver, much like a satellite dish. Our faces contain most of the receptive equipment in our bodies, so it is only natural that we should tilt our faces towards the channel of information.

When you have established eye and face contact with your speaker, you must then *react to the speaker* by sending out non-verbal signals. Your face must move and give the range of emotions that indicate whether you are following what the speaker has to say.

By moving your face to the information, you can better concentrate on what the person is saying. Your face must become an active and contoured catcher of information. A good listener will *stop talking and use receptive language* instead. Use the *I see . . . un hunh . . . oh really* words and phrases that follow and encourage your speaker's train of thought. This forces you to react to the ideas presented, rather than the person.

Exercise 2: Blackout

This short activity is designed to give participants some experience of just how much a listener depends on the non-verbal messages in order to understand fully what someone is saying.

Phase I :

Ask the participants to choose a partner from among the other group members. Then give the following instructions: (Time 10 Minutes)

Close Your Eyes

Have a conversation on an agreed topic

Keep your eyes closed for the entire conversation.

(Tell the participant that you will stop the conversation after 5 minutes.)

Phase II :

The partners now discuss with each other how they have felt during the conversation not able to see any gestures or facial expressions, and consider which particular non-verbal cues were missed most.

The Challenge of Teaching Listening Skills:

Successful listening skills are acquired over time and with lots of practice. Teaching listening skills is one of the most difficult tasks for any teacher. Like Speaking and writing have very specific exercises that can lead to improved skills but to develop listening skill there are no such exercise. Apart from this the students have their own inhibitions, they convince themselves that they are not able to understand spoken English well and create problems for themselves.

I practically have tried this motivational analogy: Imagine you want to get in shape. You decide to begin walking at fast pace. The very first day you go out and walk for three miles. If you are lucky, you might even be able to walk the three miles. However, chances are good that you will not soon go out walking again. Fitness trainers have taught us that we must begin with little steps. Begin walking short distances and walk some as well, over time you can build up the distance. Using this approach, you'll be much more likely to continue walking and get fit. Students need to apply the same approach to listening skills. Encourage them to get a film, or listen to an English radio station, but not to watch an entire film or listen for two hours. Students should often listen, but they should listen for short periods - five to ten minutes. This should happen four or five times a week. Even if they don't understand anything, five to ten minutes is not a big deal. However, for this strategy to work, students must not expect improved understanding too quickly. If a student continues this exercise over two to three months their listening comprehension skills will greatly improve.

Do this and feel the change by acquiring those skills which were a dream.

Exercise 3 : **Listening Skills Quiz – Evaluate yourself**

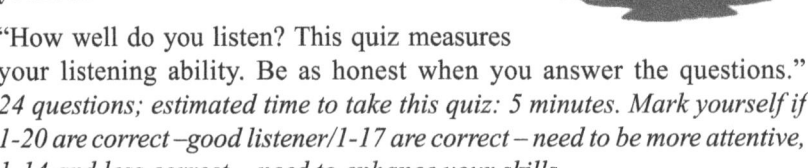

"How well do you listen? This quiz measures your listening ability. Be as honest when you answer the questions." *24 questions; estimated time to take this quiz: 5 minutes. Mark yourself if 1-20 are correct –good listener/1-17 are correct – need to be more attentive, 1-14 and less correct – need to enhance your skills*

1. While talking/listening, I like to finish sentences for others.

    Always   Usually   Sometimes   Rarly   Never

2. While talking others appear comfortable talking to me.

    Always   Usually   Sometimes   Rarly   Never

3. I sneak looks at my watch or the clock while others are talking. I often act as if they're keeping me from something that's more important.

    Always   Usually   Sometimes   Rarly   Never

4. I tend to tune out if delivery is slow or when I cannot hear the speaker.

    Always   Usually   Sometimes   Rarly   Never

5. I tend to listen for ideas rather than for facts.

    Always   Usually   Sometimes   Rarly   Never

Communication Skill 57

6. I get easily bored listening to difficult expository material.

    Always   Usually   Sometimes   Rarly   Never

7. I get distracted by other events or people in the immediate vicinity.

    Always   Usually   Sometimes   Rarly   Never

8. Whenever others approach me with a question, I immediately interrupt whatever I'm doing and give them my complete attention.

    Always   Usually   Sometimes   Rarly   Never

9. Certain emotion-laden words anger me.

    Always   Usually   Sometimes   Rarly   Never

10. I'm in the habit of cleaning my nails or fiddling with a pen, paper or paper clip, gazing at it rather than listening to the speaker.

    Always   Usually   Sometimes   Rarly   Never

11. I have a knack of steering others off their subjects with my questions and comments.

    Always   Usually   Sometimes   Rarly   Never

12. I rephrase what others say in such a way that their meanings become completely clear.

    Always   Usually   Sometimes   Rarly   Never

13. I try to anticipate waht others are going to say, then jump ahead of them to say what they had in mind.

    Always   Usually   Sometimes   Rarly   Never

14. Whenever others talk, I stare at them as if disbelieving what they have to say.

    Always   Usually   Sometimes   Rarly   Never

15. I always give the other person a chance to explain fully what his or her problems are.

    Agree   Disagree

16. I often tune out dry or uninteresting subjects.

    Agree   Disagree

17. I don't let others complete more than a few sentences before interrupting.

    Agree   Disagree

18. I never give others the feeling that they're wasting my time.

    Agree   Disagree

19. I've sometimes caught myself faking attention to the speaker.

    Agree   Disagree

20. The questions I ask about what others have just told me often indicate that I wasn't listening very well.

    Agree   Disagree

21. I always look at others while they're talking. It's not hard to tell by my attitude that I'm listening.

    Agree   Disagree

22. I try never to be flip when others have something serious to discuss.

    Agree   Disagree

23. I never put others on the defensive or confuse their thinking with my questions.

    Agree   Disagree

24. When others speak, I often look at them in an evaluative or critical way, making them wonder whether something is wrong.

    Agree   Disagree

During a job interview, a potential employer asks, "Can you take on more than one project at a time?" If you respond, "Yes," you may want to rethink that answer. According to Dynamic Listening: Interview Skills, a computer based training module from Mindleaders in Columbus, Ohio, you should avoid one-word or one-sentence answers.

Be specific. And speak money-language. Here's a preferred answer to the question above, "In general, depending upon the type and length of projects, I believe in efficiently handling more than one project at a time. This could save a company as much as 30%." Let's check out the steps of "active listening skills" and learn more to help with your next interview...

The Four Steps of Listening

Hearing is the first step in the process. At this stage, you simply pay attention to make sure you have heard the message. If your boss says, "McGillicudy, I need the CAD drawings on my desk by Friday noon," and you can repeat the sentence, then you have heard her.

The second step is interpretation. Failure to interpret the speaker's words correctly frequently leads to misunderstanding. People sometimes interpret words differently because of varying experience, knowledge, vocabulary, culture, background, and attitudes.

A good speaker uses tone of voice, facial expressions, and mannerisms to help make the message clear to the listener. For instance, if your boss speaks loudly, frowns, and puts her hands on her hips, you know she is probably upset and angry.

During the third step, evaluation, you decide what to do with the information you have received. For example, when listening to a sales pitch, you have two options: you choose either to believe or to disbelieve the salesperson. The judgments you make in the evaluation stage are a crucial part of the listening process.

The final step is to respond to what you have heard. This is a verbal or visual response that lets the speaker know whether you have gotten the message and what your reaction is. When you tell the salesperson that you want to place an order, you are showing that you have heard and believe his message.

Become a Better Listener

When it comes to listening, many of us are guilty of at least some bad habits. For example:

- Instead of listening, do you think about what you're going to say next while the other person is still talking? Engineers, thinking we know the answers and that managers do not, often tune out what non-technical speakers are saying.

- Are you easily distracted by the speaker's mannerisms or by what is going on around you?

- Do you frequently interrupt people before they have finished talking? Engineers, who value facts rather than feelings, often interrupt to set the listener straight, not realizing that the listener has a need to express himself fully, whether he is right or wrong.

- Do you drift off into daydreams because you are sure you know what the speaker is going to say? Engineers have a low tolerance level for people they assume have less knowledge than they do.
- All of these habits can hinder our listening ability. Contrary to popular notion, listening is not a passive activity. It requires full concentration and active involvement and is, in fact, hard work.

People speak at 100 to 175 words per minute (WPM), but they can listen intelligently at 600 to 800 words per minute. Since only a part of our mind is paying attention, it is easy to go into mind drift - thinking about other things while listening to someone. The cure for this is active listening - which involves listening with a purpose. It may be to gain information, obtain directions, understand others, solve problems, share interest, see how another person feels, show support, etc.

If you're finding it particularly difficult to concentrate on what someone is saying, try repeating their words mentally as they say it - this will reinforce their message and help you control mind drift.

Effective listening defined:

A process of receiving, attending, and understanding auditory messages.

Attributes of Effective listening:

- **Critical attributes**
  - Receiving
  - Attending
  - Understanding
- **Variable attributes**
  - Responding
  - Remembering

Five Types of listening

- Informative
- Relationship
- Appreciative

- Critical listening
- Discriminative

Effective listening techniques
- **Thinking about listening**
  - Understand the complexities of listening
  - Prepare to listen
  - Adjust to the situation
  - Focus on ideas and key points
  - Capitalize on speed differential
  - Organize the material for learning
- **Feeling about listening**
  - Want to listen
  - Delay judgment
  - Admit your biases
  - Don't tune out "dry" subjects
  - Accept responsibility for understanding
  - Encourage others to talk
- **Doing about listening**
  - Establish eye contact with the speaker
  - Take effective notes
  - Be a physically involved listener
  - Avoid negative mannerisms
  - Exercise your listening muscles
  - Follow the "golden rule"

What one must do to become a good listener?

1. *Don't talk. Listen.* Studies show that job applicants are more likely to make a favorable impression and get a job offer when they let the interviewer do most of the talking. This demonstrates that people appreciate a good listener more than they do a good talker.

Why is this so? Because people want a chance to get their own ideas and opinions across. A good listener lets them do it. If you interrupt the speaker or put limitations on your listening time, the speaker will get the impression that you're not interested in what he is saying — even if you are. So be courteous and give the speaker your full attention.

This technique can help you win friends, supporters, and sales. Says Dale Carnegie, "I no longer worry about being a brilliant conversationalist. I simply try to be a good listener. I notice that people who do that are usually welcome wherever they go."

2. *Don't jump to conclusions.* Many people tune out a speaker when they think they have the gist of his conversation or know what he's trying to say next. Assumptions can be dangerous. Maybe the speaker is not following the same train of thought that you are, or is not planning to make the point you think he is. If you don't listen, you may miss the real point the speaker is trying to get across.

3. *Listen "between the lines."* Concentrate on what is not being said as well as what is being said. Remember, a lot of clues to meaning come from the speaker's tone of voice, facial expressions, and gestures. People don't always say what they mean, but their body language is usually an accurate indication of their attitude and emotional state.

4. *Ask questions.* If you are not sure of what the speaker is saying, ask. It's perfectly acceptable to say, "Do you mean . . . ?" or "Did I understand you to say . . . ?" It's also a good idea to repeat what the speaker has said in your own words to confirm that you have understood him correctly.

Sometimes we engineers cling to the mistaken notion that if it's technical, we are expected to know it. But with the explosion of technology and information, that's impossible. As Thomas Edison said, **"We don't know one millionth of one percent about anything." The only way you learn is by listening and asking questions.**

5. *Don't let yourself be distracted by the environment or by the speaker's appearance, accent, mannerisms, or word use.* It's sometimes difficult to overlook a strong accent, a twitch, sexist language, a fly buzzing around the speaker's head, and similar

distractions. But paying too much attention to these distributions can break your concentration and make you miss the point of the conversation.

If outside commotion is a problem, try to position yourself away from it. Make eye contact with the speaker, and force yourself to focus on the message, not the environment.

Keep an open mind. Don't just listen for statements that back up your own opinions and support your beliefs, or for certain parts that interest you. The point of listening, after all, is to gain new information.

Be willing to listen to someone else's point of view and ideas. A subject that may seem boring or trivial at first can turn out to be fascinating, if you listen with an open mind.

On the average, you can think four times faster than the listener can talk. So, when listening, use this extra brainpower to evaluate what has been said and summarize the central ideas in your own mind.

That way, you'll be better prepared to answer any questions or criticisms the speaker poses, and you'll be able to discuss the topic much more effectively.

6. *Provide feedback.* Make eye contact with the speaker. Show him you understand his talk by nodding your head, maintaining an upright posture, and, if appropriate, interjecting an occasional comment such as ''I see'' or "that's interesting" or "really." The speaker will appreciate your interest and feel that you are really listening.

Tips for Better Listening

- Control external and internal distractions.
- Become actively involved.
- Identify important facts.
- Don't interrupt.
- Ask clarifying questions.
- Paraphrase to increase understanding.
- Take advantage of lag time.
- Take notes to ensure retention

Behaviors that *support* effective listening
- Maintaining relaxed body posture
- Leaning slightly forward if sitting
- Facing person squarely at eye level
- Maintaining an open posture
- Maintaining appropriate distance
- Offering simple acknowledgments
- Reflecting meaning (paraphrase)
- Reflecting emotions
- Using eye contact

Behaviors that *hinder* effective listening
- Acting distracted
- Telling your own story without acknowledging theirs first
- No response
- Invalidating response, put downs
- Interrupting
- Criticizing
- Judging
- Diagnosing
- Giving advice/solutions
- Changing the subject
- Reassuring without acknowledgment

Exercise 4 Self Evaluation Exercise On Listening Skills

How well you and your partner listen is critical to effective communication. Effective communication is the life-blood of all good relationships.

This listening skills rating is a self-evaluation of the current level of your listening skills as well as what you perceive your partner's listening skills to be. Please complete the form at this time and, if your partner is working along with you, he/she should do so as well. Take the evaluations separately, review the scoring which follows on a page indicated at the bottom, and then get together to discuss the results. We suggest that you print the evaluations and complete them on paper so you will have print copies to compare. Be sure to keep an open mind so you may learn and grow.

INSTRUCTIONS : Think about how often **you** do the following and write in the number that you think matches that frequency?

On a scale from 1 to 5, give yourself a score as follows: 1 = never, 2 = rarely, 3 = sometimes, 4 = often, 5 = very often.

Behaviour	Score
I avoid staying on any one subject with my partner	
I make assumptions about my partners feelings or thoughts.	
I respond to my partner's suggestions or opinions with, "Yes, but…"	
I bring up past issues during current disagreements.	
I interrupt my partner's conversation.	
I use sarcasm or jokes to respond when my partner talks	
I respond to a complaint with a complaint.	
I insult and criticize my partner.	
I respond to my partner with phrases like, "That's ridiculous."	
I see only my point of view.	
TOTAL (Add up your scores.)	

Now *You* rate your *partner's* listening skills: How often do they do the following?

On a scale from 1 to 5, give them a score as follows: 1 = never, 2 = rarely, 3 = sometimes, 4 = often, 5 = very often

Behaviour	Score
My partner avoids staying on a subject until it is solved	
My partner make assumptions about my feelings or thoughts.	
My partner comments with, "Yes, but..." to my suggestions or opinions.	
My partner brings up past issues during current disagreements.	
My partner interrupts my conversation.	
My partner use sarcasm or jokes to respond when I talk.	
My partner responds to my complaints with a complaint.	
My partner insults and criticizes me	
My partner responds to me with phrases like, "That's ridiculous."	
My partner see only their point of view.	
TOTAL (Add up your scores for your partner.)	

Discussion : Make a note of the total scores for yourself and your partner

> **Exercise 5:**
>
> Sit still for about five minutes with your eyes shut. Concentrate on the things you can hear, and identify as many different sounds as you can. At the end of the five minutes make a list, independently, of these sounds. Finally, discuss the results with your partner. What conclusion can be drawn about listening?

THE WAY TO BUILD COMMUNICATION SKILLS

- **Read newspapers and magazines to learn how to have well-informed conversations.** Staying current on the latest news and topics of general interest gives you the ability to converse intelligently with others.
- **Go to a movie or play with someone and then discuss it to learn how to persuade people to your point of view.** Debating the merits and content of a movie or play with others allows you to explore some of the more abstract aspects of a topic. Without realizing it, you are learning about persuasive speaking

- **Start or join a book club to learn how to connect your thoughts and opinions to someone else's ideas.** What's good about this suggestion is that: 1. You pick the book; and 2. You decide what you want to discuss. Regardless of the books or subjects, you practice connecting your thoughts and opinions to someone else's work.
- **Volunteer for campus or community organizations to learn how to empathize with your audience.** The more variety of people you have contact with, the better your communication skills become.
- **Talk to people in industry to learn how to organize your thoughts.** By speaking with people in industry, you find out how they use language, how they organize their thoughts and how they communicate information about fields they know well.
- **Read, read, read to learn basic speaking and writing skills.** It doesn't matter what you read — novels, magazines, newspapers, reports, technical papers. The more you read, the more you know, and the more effectively you will speak and write.
- **Give presentations in class to practice public speaking.** Take advantage of every opportunity to give oral presentations in class, any class. This is a great exercise, and you will never get fired from college if your presentation isn't perfect.
- **Contribute articles to school or department publications to learn concise writing.** One great way to master how to communicate is to write about something you believe in and make it comply with guidelines set by an editor. You also learn to accept criticism by having your document edited.
- **Socialize to learn how to listen, organize your thoughts, respect others' opinions and present your ideas.** This may sound a little too obvious, but think back to the last time you had a substantial conversation with someone and talked about a topic that was really important to both of you. Having an in-depth conversation forces you to listen, organize your thoughts, respect the other person's opinion and present your ideas clearly.

Speaking Skills

Imagine if Nathan Hale had said, **"Okay, I'm willing to die for my country,"** instead of "I regret that I have but one life to give for my country." Imagine Franklin D. Roosevelt saying **"Don't be afraid,"** instead of "We have nothing to fear but fear itself." Imagine John F. Kennedy saying **"Do good things for your country,"** instead of "Ask not what your country can do for you, but what you can do for your country!"

The words themselves make the difference in the intensity of the message, even when we no longer hear the tonality or see the body language with which they were spoken.

Consider the following question: What was your favorite subject in school?

- ☺ Math?
- ☺ Science?
- ☺ Social Studies?
- ☺ Music?
- ☺ Gym?
- ☺ English?

Did you answer English? Most folks don't. That's a problem because English skills transfer most directly into the business world. You reveal your English expertise—or more typically lack thereof—every time you write or speak. Whenever you greet a person, make a comment, present a proposal, reply to a phone call, leave a voice mail, jot a note, write a letter, or send an e-mail, whatever your career, you are communicating with your image at stake.

Communicating quickly, clearly, and correctly creates a golden image that saves, even earns, you money. A tarnished image costs you!

How golden are your writing, grammar, and speaking skills?

Engineers need it more than anybody else. Engineers are used to working around machines & computers. They need to develop their Language skills. They need this skill to present their Technical/Non-Technical matters impressively and interestingly.

Why? What?

Impact on Career Progression

Question: Can you succeed technically without these skills?

Great technical skills, weak communications skills----------

Destined for "back room" engineering positions

Will not advance up the technical career ladder

Great communications skills, less technical

Very strong leaders if able to effectively leverage technical team members

Strong technical and communications skills

Rising Stars!!!

Almost everyone experiences some degree of nervousness when they have to be a "speaker," whether it is a formal presentation in front of a group twenty-five, presenting information to someone "important," or being called on in a meeting to answer a question. Your heart starts pounding loudly, your throat constricts, the face feels hot and you're on.

There are 4 key skills when you learn a language: listening, speaking, reading, writing. Which one of these is the "Odd-One-Out"? Which one of these is different from the other three? The answer is speaking. The other three you can do alone, on your own, without anyone else. You can listen to the radio alone. You can read a book alone. You can write a letter alone. But you can't really speak alone! Speaking to yourself can be "dangerous" because men in white coats may come and take you away!! That is why you should make every effort possible to find somebody to speak with.

New communication technologies and possibilities, combined with new challenges confronting organizations, are encouraging a whole new approach to organizational communication that challenges the very nature of organizations themselves

Oral Communication is a basic tool of professional and business interaction. One should be able to use it fluently and confidently. The growth and expansion of service oriented industry has also increased the significance of oral competence for professional in different fields. Good speaking skill has become more acute requirement for a student. Seeing the JOB Advertisement one would find that COMMUNICATION has become "The Want" for any company and for one's career

Speaking in varied forms
Conference

"Makes a ready man"

Getting your message across is paramount to progressing. To do this, you must understand what your message is, what audience you are sending it to, and how it will be perceived. You must also weigh-in the circumstances surrounding your communications, such as situational and cultural context.

A one to one conference is a conversation
A one to a small group is called briefing.
A one to many is called addressing.

The Aim of addressing / briefing is to share information or enthuse or motivate many.

Be prepared.
Look interested.
Speak up.
Ask questions.
Do not be defensive.
Build on ideas you have heard.
Support each other.
Pay attention to what is said.
Have a sense of humor – it enhances approachability, helps build team cohesion. Use a smile.

Presentation

"The human brain starts working the moment you are born and never stops until you stand up to speak in public."

With these words, George Jessel captured a sentiment people feel their entire lives: they dread the very thought of speaking in public. The original Book of lists speaking before a group as the single worst human fear. (Fear of dying is sixth!)

For those who want to conquer this common fear and those who already speak in front of groups but would like to do so with greater ease and effectiveness, this book is designed to put participants at ease while challenging them to apply concepts they're learning (yes, by actually speaking), this book gives participants essential tools for affecting others with their sales presentations, public speeches, presentations at meetings, or other speaking opportunities

It is a simple fact that a great idea will always lose out to a great presentation and the only way to deliver a great presentation is to have presentation skills. Few people (if any) are "born presenters." Some, of course, have the "gift of gab" but that gift doesn't substitute for presentation skills.

"There are always three speeches, for every one you actually gave. The one you practiced, the one you gave, and the one you wish you gave."

- Dale Carnegie

The long-standing theatre phrase "Illusion of the First Time" means that when an actor performs in a play for the 10th, 100th or 1,000th time, he or she must create the illusion that this is the first time the actor has said these words, used these expressions or made these movements. The audience wants and expects an aura of freshness.

> Something like this
>
> **I Have A Dream!** Or how about Martin Luther King, defying the current conditions of his time and declaring to the world, "I Have A Dream." King met race, religion and raging emotions with his passion to communicate one on one or to the audiences he held spellbound, in whatever manner that was useful for his desired outcomes

Likewise, superlative speakers need to give an obviously "live" presentation. No matter how many times you have talked about this topic previously, today's audience is hearing you for the first time.

> People make judgments about you based on how you speak. Your speech affects your credibility and even how intelligent you are seen as being.
>
> I recently watched a presentation where the speaker used "uh," "umm" and other verbal fillers more than 37 times in 10 minutes. I counted. He fidgeted, put his hands in his pockets and looked completely uncomfortable. He knew his subject, but his nervous mannerisms made him appear less than credible.
>
> Fillers, tics and nervous mannerisms are most common when speaking in front of a group, but they can creep in to your daily conversations, too. At the airport, I overheard two women having a business conversation and I was astounded at how often they used the word "like."
>
> If you catch yourself using "like," "uh," "you know," etc., it usually means that you are stalling for time to think of your next word. Slow down. Take a breath. Think about what you're saying.
>
> Ask a friend to signal you when you slip into one of your bad habits.
>
> Record yourself speaking in different situations and listen to how you sound.
>
> Concentrate on removing one bad habit at a time. Trying to fix everything at once may make you more nervous and self-conscious when you speak.

74   Essential Key for Corporate Threshold

Presentations are one of the first managerial skills which a junior engineer must acquire. This article looks at the basics of Presentation Skills as they might apply to an emergent manager.

- Fending off the panic (Ugh!)
- Getting started means getting clear about your purpose
- Sizing up your audience and the situation to organize your ideas
- Planning to capture and keep audience attention
- Closing with power and ensuring they'll remember
- Arranging the room to your advantage
- Using body language and your voice (presentation techniques)
- Reading and working a room (responding to body language)
- Answering tough questions and listening effectively
- Maintaining control
- Designing and using easy visual aids
- Creating and using memory aids
- Speaking impromptu

As engineers, it is vitally important to be able to communicate your thoughts and ideas effectively, using a variety of tools and medium. You will need to develop and use this skill throughout your years in University; when you attend job interviews and especially when you start working in the big wide world. But, it is often said that engineers do not possess the ability to communicate well. Of course that is a load of b*&%@ks - not enough coaching and practise that's all!

Two areas of concern for speakers are what to say (content) and how to say it (delivery). A typical process often followed before presenting includes protesting, procrastinating, panicking, and praying. Yes, praying helps, but we recommend replacing the other three steps with planning, practicing, and polishing instead. This proven three-step process helps speakers experience decreased fear along with increased competence and confidence when designing and delivering powerful presentations

The Objectives of Communication

The single most important observation is that the objective of communication is not the transmission but the reception. The whole preparation, presentation and content of a speech must therefore be geared not to the speaker but to the audience. The presentation of a perfect project plan is a failure if the audience do not understand or are not persuaded of its merits. A customers' tour is a waste of time if they leave without realizing the full worth of your product. The objective of communication is to make your message understood and remembered.

The main problem with this objective is, of course, the people to whom you are talking. The average human being has a very short attention span and a million other things to think about. Your job in the presentation is to reach through this mental fog and to hold the attention long enough to make your point.

Communication is always the link that will be used to negotiate the issue/argument whether it is face-to-face, on the telephone or in writing. Remember, negotiation is not always between two people: it can involve several members from two parties. Negotiation is something that we do all the time and is not only used for business purposes. For example, we use it in our social lives perhaps for deciding a time to meet, or where to go on a rainy day.

The Plan

It is difficult to over estimate the importance of careful preparation. Five minutes on the floor in front of senior management could decide the acceptance of a proposal of several months duration for the manager and

76   Essential Key for Corporate Threshold

the whole team. With so much potentially at stake, the presenter must concentrate not only upon the facts being presented but upon the style, pace, tone and ultimately tactics which should be used. As a rule of thumb for an average presentation, no less than 1 hour should be spent in preparation for 5 minutes of talking.

Suppose you have a talk to give, where do you start?

Clear plan is vital to effective speaking. The most prevalent weakness among speakers at all levels is the failure to organize material for the audience. Speakers have the responsibility to lead listeners mentally from where they are at the beginning of a talk to where they are supposed to be at the end. The message must be planned with the audience in mind; the organization should conform to the thinking processes and expectations of the listeners.

Each speech, lecture, and briefing needs an introduction, a body, and a conclusion. In most instances the introduction and conclusion should be prepared after the body of the talk, since the material in the body is a guide for preparing the introduction and conclusion.

The first consideration in planning the body is how to organize the main points, but organization of subpoints is also important. Arrangement of the main points and subpoints will help both the speaker and the audience remember the material—the speaker while speaking, and the audience while listening.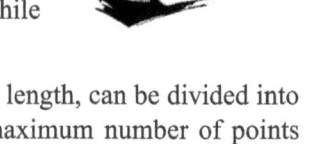

Most oral presentations, regardless of their length, can be divided into two to five main points. Five is about the maximum number of points from one talk that listeners can be expected to remember.

The most typical ways of organizing main points or subpoints of a talk are by the patterns: time, space, cause/effect, problem/solution, pro/con, or topic.

Now that You Have Planned

The organization patterns and strategies you choose provide structure to the body of your talk. But structure without content is not enough. Interesting and effective supporting material is needed.

Formulate your Objectives

Preparing your presentation is the key to how successful it will be. Write a plan of how you will structure your presentation from beginning to end. The starting point in planning any speech is to formulate a precise objective. This should take the form of a simple, concise statement of intent. For example, the purpose of your speech may be to obtain funds, to evaluate a proposal, or to motivate your team. No two objectives will be served equally well by the same presentation; and if you are not sure at the onset what you are trying to do, it is unlikely that your plan will achieve it.

Keep in mind the amount of time you have and be sure that you won't exceed this. Not using all the time is better than running out, and therefore unable to cover all areas. The best advice is to be brief or you will lose the audiences' interest if you go into too much detail. Think through, and write down in as much detail as you can, all that you want to cover.

One question is: how many different objectives can you achieve, in say, 30 minutes - and the answer: not many. In the end it is far more productive to achieve one goal than to blunder over several. The best approach is to isolate the essential objective and to list at most two others which can be addressed providing they do not distract from the main one. *Focus is key*. If you do not focus upon your objective, it is unlikely that the audience will.

Identify the Audience

The next task is to consider the audience to determine how best to achieve your objectives in the context of these people. Essentially this is done by identifying their aims and objectives while attending your presentation. If you can somehow convince them they are achieving those aims while at the same time achieving your own, you will find a helpful and receptive audience. For instance, if you are seeking approval for a new product plan from senior management it is useful to know and understand their main objectives. If they are currently worried that their product range

is out of date and old fashioned, you would emphasize the innovative aspects of your new product; if they are fearful about product diversification you would then emphasize how well your new product fits within the existing catalogue.

This principal of matching the audience aims, however, goes beyond the simple salesmanship of an idea - it is the simplest and most effective manner of obtaining their attention at the beginning. If your opening remarks imply that you understand their problem and that you have a solution, then they will be flattered at your attention and attentive to your every word.

Structure

All speeches should have a definite structure or format; a talk without a structure is a woolly mess. If you do not order your thoughts into a structured manner, the audience will not be able to follow them. Having established the aim of your presentation you should choose the most appropriate structure to achieve it.

However, the structure must not get in the way of the main message. If it is too complex, too convoluted or simply too noticeable the audience will be distracted. If a section is unnecessary to the achievement of your fundamental objectives, pluck it out.

Sequential Argument

One of the simplest structures is that of sequential argument which consists of a series of linked statements ultimately leading to a conclusion. However, this simplicity can only be achieved by careful and deliberate delineation between each section. One technique is the use of frequent reminders to the audience of the main point which have proceeded and explicit explanation of how the next topic will lead on from this.

Hierarchical Decomposition

In hierarchical decomposition the main topic is broken down into sub-topics and each sub-topics into smaller topics until eventually everything is broken down into very small basic units. In written communication this is a very powerful technique because it allows the reader to re-order the presentation at will, and to return to omitted topics at a later date. In verbal communication the audience is restricted to the order of the presenter and the hierarchy should be kept simple reinforced. As with sequential argument it is useful to summarise each section at its conclusion and to introduce each major new section with a statement of how it lies in the hierarchical order.

Humorous Oriented

The perfect start is to 'win' the audiences' interest by using a dramatic statement, humour or a prop (model, poster, etc): humour is always risky – clever humour is deadly. You can keep their interest during the presentation by involving them, like asking questions or a simple vote (vote: much under used to gain involvement).There are many benefits you can derive from using humor in your presentations. Keep in mind that these benefits only help you reach your ultimate purpose for making the presentation. They are not purposes themselves unless, of course, you are only interested in entertaining. Using humor does the following for you:

HELPS YOU CONNECT WITH THE AUDIENCE.

- Makes you more likeable.
- Arouses interest.
- Keeps attention.
- Helps emphasize points and ideas.
- Disarms hostility
- Overcomes overly flattering introductions.
- Gets your point across without creating hostility.
- Helps relate facts and figures.
- Makes a positive impression.
- Shows that you don't take yourself too seriously.
- Helps paint pictures in the audience's mind.
- Makes information more memorable.
- Lightens up heavy material.

Question Orientated

The aim of many presentations given by managers is to either explain a previous decision or to seek approval for a plan of action. In these cases, the format can be question orientated. The format is to introduce the problem and any relevant background, and then to outline the various solutions to that problem listing the advantages and disadvantages of each solution in turn. Finally, all possible options are summarized in terms of their pro's and con's, and either the preferred solution is presented for endorsement by the audience or a discussion is initiated leading to the decision. One trick for obtaining the desired outcome is to establish during the presentation the criteria by which the various options are to be judged; this alone should allow you to obtain your desired outcome.

Pyramid

In a newspaper, the story is introduced in its entirety in a catchy first paragraph. The next few paragraphs repeat the same information only giving further details to each point. The next section repeats the entire story again, but developing certain themes within each of the sub-points and again adding more information. This is repeated until the reporter runs out of story. The editor then simply decides upon the newsworthiness of the report and cuts from the bottom to the appropriate number of column inches.

There are two main advantages to this style for presentations. Firstly, it can increase the audiences receptiveness to the main ideas. Since at every stage of the pyramid they have all ready become familiar with the ideas and indeed know what to expect next. This sense of *deja vu* can falsely give the impression that what they are hearing are their own ideas. The second advantage is that the duration of the talk can be easily altered by cutting the talk in exactly the same way as the newspaper editor might have done to the news story. This degree of flexibility may be useful if the same presentation is to be used several times in different situations.

The Meaty Sandwich

The simplest and most direct format remains the meaty sandwich. This is the simple beginning-middle-end format in which the main meat of the exposition is contained in the middle and is proceeded by an introduction and followed by a summary and conclusion. This is really the appropriate format for all small sub-sections in all the previous structures. If the talk is short enough, or the topic simple enough, it can indeed form the entirety of the presentation.

The Beginning

It is imperative to plan your beginning carefully; there are five main elements:

1. *Get their attention :* Too often in a speech, the first few minutes of the presentation are lost while people adjust their coats, drift in with coffee and finish the conversation they were having with the person next to them. We all have short attention spans. This is exacerbated in these days of communication delivered in truncated, rapid-fire bytes. So when you are designing your presentation you need to factor in frequent ways to keep your audience's attention You only

have a limited time and every minute is precious to you so, from the beginning, make sure they pay attention.

2. *Establish a theme :* Basically, you need to start the audience thinking about the subject matter of your presentation. This can be done by a statement of your main objective, unless for some reason you wish to keep it hidden. They will each have some experience or opinions on this and at the beginning you must make them bring that experience into their own minds.

Present a structure

If you explain briefly at the beginning of a talk how it is to proceed, then the audience will know what to expect. This can help to establish the theme and also provide something concrete to hold their attention. Ultimately, it provides a sense of security in the promise that this speech too will end.

3. *Create a rapport :* If you can win the audience over in the first minute, you will keep them for the remainder. You should plan exactly how you wish to appear to them and use the beginning to establish that relationship. You may be presenting yourself as their friend, as an expert, perhaps even as a judge, but whatever role you choose you must establish it at the very beginning.

And now we are back to how to "speak publicly and enjoy!" Because it all begins…and ends… with or ability to speak effectively, first with ourselves, and then with others. No matter the size or occasion of the "group.

Now, if boosting and accelerating your skills to reach and move others is important to you, you can find someone to model…someone that has the skill set, beliefs and values that you desire to acquire.

A number of years ago I began to model Carmine Baffa, Ph.D, someone who has literally mastered the art of communicating with integrity, wisdom and effectiveness. And mastered it on levels that will shock you. I have seen Carmine Baffa, Ph.D, creator of Human Performance Engineering ™ hold individuals and groups, small and large, in the palm of his hand, time after time after time…simply put, when Carmine enters a room, everything changes.

> **Why?** In part, because Carmine has the ability to have rapport with anyone he desires to have rapport with. Children, adolescents, adults, it does not matter. Female, male, it does not matter. C.E.O, parent, gang member, millionaire, penniless and homeless, it does not matter. Why not give yourself the opportunity to model someone who does this on a routine basis?
>
> **The fact is that Carmine operates from a place of deep caring and respect for each person that comes into his space. And when they are in his space, he exists for them, and them alone. He marshals his vast experience, his skill, his genius, to give to that person or group what they are most needing at the time. And nothing will stop him from doing just that. Just ask me sometime about what I have witnessed to this effect. But that's Carmine.**
>
> **What about you?**
>
> **Begin today! Take a step in the direction of your dreams. Why? Because you can.**

4. *Administration :* When planning your speech you should make a note to find out if there are any administrative details which need to be announced at the beginning of your speech. This is not simply to make yourself popular with the people organising the session but also because if these details are over looked the audience may become distracted as they wonder what is going to happen next.

5. *The Ending :* The final impression you make on the audience is the one they will remember. Thus it is worth planning your last few sentences with extreme care.

   As with the beginning, it is necessary first to get their attention, which will have wandered.

   This requires a change of pace, a new visual aid or perhaps the introduction of one final culminating idea.

In some formats the ending will be a summary of the main points of the talk.

Indeed it is best that the ending comes unexpectedly with that final vital phrase left hanging in the air and ringing round their memories. Alternatively the ending can be a flourish, with the pace and voice leading the audience through the final crescendo to the inevitable conclusion.

Visual Aids

Introduce a new visual. Challenge with an activity for audience involvement. Tell a story. Whatever techniques you use, introduce them often and vary them. Each will have its own impact, but make sure that impact supports your chosen image and message.

Most people expect visual reinforcement for any verbal message being delivered.

Firstly, you can meet their expectations using the overhead projector, a slide show, or even a video presentation; secondly, if you depart from the framework of a square picture flashed before their eyes, and use a different format, then that novelty will be most arresting.

For instance, if you are describing the four functions of a project manager then display the four "hats" he/she must wear; if you are introducing the techniques of brainstorming then brandish a fishing rod to "fish for" ideas.

As with all elements of a speech, each different viewfoil should have a distinct purpose - and if it has no purpose it should be removed. With that purpose firmly in mind you should design the viewfoil for that purpose. Some viewfoils are there to reinforce the verbal message and so to assist in recall; others are used to explain information which can be more easily displayed than discussed: and some viewfoils are designed simply for entertainment and thus to pace the presentation.

The data should be extracted before being displayed. Talk to the audience, not the visual aid.

The Delivery

"The human body is truly fascinating - there are some I could watch all day" - Anon

Break up the presentation, while reinforcing your message is to **consider learning styles**. People will (usually) happily sit through a presentation that does not fit their learning style but they will have a sense of disconnection. They may understand your message, recognise the quality of your presentation and absorb your image, but the communication will be incomplete and the audience members will feel disconnected. If you can communicate using their personal learning style the impact will be far, far greater. There is a myriad of books and websites for you, on learning styles. Basically, you can work with three – visual, auditory and kinesthetic. Delivering your message verbally will work for the auditory learners, but you will reinforce it even further if you can get them to talk as well – to hear themselves and others repeat and supplement the ideas. Create as many visuals as you can for the visual learners – use diagrams to show difficult concepts, pictures to reinforce concrete ideas and colours to support emotional impact. And for the kinesthetic learners – give them ways to learn by doing, if only discussing ideas or writing them down. Then each group has received your message in a way that will make it slot into their brains and experience banks with ease.

Whatever you say and whatever you show; it is you, yourself which will remain the focus of the audience's attention.

The presenter has the power both to kill the message and to enhance it a hundred times beyond its worth.

Your job as a manager is to use the potential of the presentation to ensure that the audience is motivated and inspired rather than disconcerted or distracted.

There are five key facets of the human body which deserve attention in presentation skills: the eyes, the voice, the expression, the appearance, and how you stand.

> **What's Wrong With My Presentation?**
>
> "That meeting was just a waste of time!"
>
> "I just spent 45 minutes with him and still have no idea what I'm supposed to do!"
>
> "That was the most boring presentation I've ever heard!"
>
> "It took her 15 minutes to answer the question when all I needed was a simple yes or no"
>
> If you've ever heard (or said) any of those statements, then the problem is obvious: the presenters lack the effective presentation skills to communicate their ideas to others

The Eyes

The eyes are said to be the key to the soul and are therefore the first and most effective weapon in convincing the audience of your honesty, openness and confidence in the objectives of your presentation.

During the presentation you should use this to enhance your rapport with the audience by establishing eye contact with each and every member of the audience as often as possible. For small groups this is clearly possible but it can also be achieved in large auditoriums since the further the audience is away from the presenter the harder it is to tell precisely where he or she is looking.

During presentations, try to hold your gaze fixed in specific directions for five or six seconds at a time. Shortly after each change in position, a slight smile will convince each person in that direction that you have seen and acknowledged them.

The Voice

After the eyes comes the voice, and the two most important aspects of the voice for the public speaker are projection and variation. It is important to realise from the onset that few people can take their ordinary conversation voice and put it on stage

In ordinary conversation you can see from the expression, perhaps a subtle movement of the eye, when a word or phrase has been missed or misunderstood. In front of an audience you have to make sure that this never happens. The simple advice is to slow down and to take your time.

A safe style is to be slightly louder and slightly slower than a fire-side chat with slightly deaf aunt. As you get used to the sound, you can adjust it by watching the audience.

A monotone speech is both boring and soporific, so it is important to try to vary the pitch and speed of your presentation.

At the very least, each new sub-section should be proceeded by a pause and a change in tone to emphasize the delineation..

Expression

The audience watch your face. If you are looking listless or distracted then they will be listless and distracted; if you are smiling, they will be wondering why and listen to find out. In normal conversation your meaning is enhanced by facial reinforcement. Thus in a speech you must compensate both for stage nerves and for the distance between yourself and the audience. The message is quite simply: make sure that your facial expressions are natural, only more so.

Appearance

There are many guides to management and presentation styles which lay heavy emphasis upon the way you dress and in the last analysis this is a matter of personal choice. That choice should however be deliberately made. When you are giving a presentation you must dress for the audience, not for yourself; if they think you look out of place, then you are.

As an aside, it is my personal opinion that there exists a code of conduct among engineers which emphasizes the scruffy look, and that in many organisations this tends to set the engineer apart, especially from management. It conveys the subliminal message that the engineer and the manager are not part of the same group and so hinders communication.

Stance

When an actor initially learns a new character part, he or she will instinctively adopt a distinct posture or stance to convey that character. It follows therefore that while you are on stage, your stance and posture will convey a great deal about you. The least you must do is make sure your stance does not convey boredom; at best, you can use your whole body as a dynamic tool to reinforce your rapport with the audience.

The perennial problem is what to do with your hands. These must not wave aimlessly through the air, or fiddle constantly with a pen, or (worst of all visually) juggle change in your trouser pockets. The key is to keep your hands still, except when used in unison with your speech. To train them initially, find a safe resting place which is comfortable for you, and aim to return them there when any gesture is completed.

The Techniques of Speech

Every speaker has a set of "tricks of the trade" which he or she holds dear- the following are a short selection of such advice taken from various sources.

Make an impression

The average audience is very busy: they have husbands and wives, schedules and slippages, cars and mortgages; and although they will be trying very hard to concentrate on your speech, their minds will inevitably stray. Your job is to do something, anything, which captures their attention and makes a lasting impression upon them. Once you have planned your speech and honed it down to its few salient points, isolate the most important and devise some method to make it stick.

Repeat, Repeat

The average audience is very busy: they have husbands or wives etc, etc- but repetition makes them hear. The average audience is easily distracted, and their attention will slip during the most important message of your speech - so repeat it.

The classic advice of the Sergeant Major is: "First you tell 'em what you are going to tell 'em, then you tell 'em, then you tell 'em what you told 'em!"

Draw a Picture

use metaphors or analogies to express your message. Thus a phrase like "we need to increase the market penetration before there will be sufficient profits for a pay related bonus" becomes "we need a bigger slice of the cake before the feast".

Jokes

You must choose a joke which is apt, and one which will not offend any member of the audience..

Amusing asides are also useful in maintaining the attention of the audience, and for relieving the tension of the speech.

The Narrative

Everyone loves a story and stories can both instruct and convey a message: Zen Philosophy is recorded in its stories, and Christianity was originally taught in parables. If you can weave your message into a story or a personal annocdote, then you can have them wanting to hear your every word - even if you have to make it up.

Rehearsal

There is no substitute for rehearsal. You can do it in front of a mirror, or to an empty theatre. In both cases, you should accentuate your gestures and vocal projection so that you get used to the sound and sight of yourself.

Relaxation

If you get nervous just before the show, either concentrate on controlling your breathing or welcome the extra adrenaline. If you dry-up in the middle - *smile*, look at your notes, and take your time. The silence will seem long to you, but less so to the audience.

Conclusion

Once the speech is over and you have calmed down, you should try to honestly evaluate your performance. Either alone, or with the help of a friend in the audience, decide what was the least successful aspect of your presentation and resolve to concentrate on that point in the next talk you give. If it is a problem associated with the preparation, then deal with it there; if it is a problem with your delivery, write yourself a reminder note and put it in front of you at the next talk

Tips and Techniques For Great Presentations

Eleanor was a shy young girl who was terrified at the thought of speaking in public. But with each passing year, she grew in confidence and self-esteem. She once said, "No one can make you feel inferior, unless you agree with it."

- If you have handouts, do not read straight from them. The audience does not know if they should read along with you or listen to you read.
- Do not put both hands in your pockets for long periods of time. This tends to make you look unprofessional. It is OK to put one hand in a pocket but ensure there is no loose change or keys to jingle around. This will distract the listeners.
- Do not wave a pointer around in the air like a wild knight branding a sword to slay a dragon. Use the pointer for what it is intended and then put it down, otherwise the audience will become fixated upon your "sword", instead upon you.
- Do not lean on the podium for long periods. The audience will begin to wonder when you are going to fall over.
- Speak to the audience...NOT to the visual aids, such as flip charts or overheads. Also, do not stand between the visual aid and the audience.
- Speak clearly and loudly enough for all to hear. Do not speak in a monotone voice. Use inflection to emphasize your main points.
- The disadvantages of presentations is that people cannot see the punctuation and this can lead to misunderstandings. An effective way of overcoming this problem is to pause at the time when there would normally be punctuation marks.
- Use colored backgrounds on overhead transparencies and slides (such as yellow) as the bright white light can be harsh on the eyes. This will quickly cause your audience to tire. If all of your transparencies or slides have clear backgrounds, then tape one blank yellow one on the overhead face. For slides, use a rubber band to hold a piece of colored cellophane over the projector lens.

- Learn the name of each participant as quickly as possible. Based upon the atmosphere you want to create, call them by their first names or by using Mr., Mrs., Miss, Ms.
- Tell them what name and title you prefer to be called.
- Listen intently to comments and opinions. By using a *lateral thinking technique* (adding to ideas rather than dismissing them), the audience will feel that their ideas, comments, and opinions are worthwhile.
- Circulate around the room as you speak. This movement creates a physical closeness to the audience.
- List and discuss your objectives at the beginning of the presentation. Let the audience know how your presentation fits in with their goals. Discuss some of the fears and apprehensions that both you and the audience might have. Tell them what they should expect of you and how you will contribute to their goals.
- Vary your techniques (lecture, discussion, debate, films, slides, reading, etc.)
- Get to the presentation before your audience arrives; be the last one to leave.
- Be prepared to use an alternate approach if the one you've chosen seems to bog down. You should be confident enough with your own material so that the audience's interests and concerns, not the presentation outline, determines the format. Use your background, experience, and knowledge to interrelate your subject matter.
- When writing on flip charts use no more than 7 lines of text per page and no more than 7 word per line (the 7 7 rule). Also, use bright and bold colors, and pictures as well as text.
- Consider the time of day and how long you have got for your talk. Time of day can affect the audience. After lunch is known as the graveyard section in training circles as audiences will feel more like a nap than listening to a talk.
- Most people find that if they practice in their head, the actual talk will take about 25 per cent longer. Using a flip chart or other visual aids also adds to the time. Remember - **it is better to finish slightly early than to overrun.**

Communication Skill   91

The success of industries depends on the young, energetic and skilled technocrats, armed with modern know-how and global trends of technical education. Apart from the excellence of technical education, a technocrat must posses a well-balanced personality, kindled with ethical, moral & human values. In this highly competitive world to get a right person for the right job is not an easy task. There has been a colossal demand for Fresh Engineers that has far exceeded its supply.

Employers are always on a hunt for Engineers who can generate innovative ideas with the right attitude, aptitude and skills. In this world of fierce competition, getting a job is by no means an easy task. Endless queues of educated youth strive to find a foothold in the corporate world.

A job interview is similar in many ways to a social conversation, but it requires more than just conversational skills. How well you do in a job interview will depend on how well you can elaborate on your accomplishments and qualifications as they relate to what the employer wants and needs.

> **"An interview is a meeting of persons for discussion where there is an explicit objective to the conversation and where one party is responsible for achieving this objective."**
> Janis Grummit, *A Guide to Interviewing Skills, The Industrial Society, 1980*

Interviewing

Just because you have a college degree, even if it's from a top-notch Ivy League Institute, nobody awes you anything. If you're not willing to put forth the effort to get yourself a great job and then succeed in that position, then it's nobodies fault but your own if you wind up in a boring, dead-end job. Sorry, but that's how the real world operates, and if you go into the real world understanding this, you've got a much better chance for success. What ever you do, never give up and don't settle.

Among personal qualities possessed by college graduates the ability to communicate effectively was ranked first by employers.

From a survey of 480 companies and public organizations conducted by the National Association of Colleges and Employers.

WSJ, Dec 29, 1999

I know from personal experience that the job search can be a very confusing, frustrating, and frightening time in someone's life. After all you're going from the structured and protected environment of education, and probably for the first time in your life, you're being forced to make decisions that will impact the rest of your life. Now that's menacing, if you have no clue about what type of career you want to pursue. Despite what you've been told by educators, your parents, your friends, and others, if you're thinking that you have to "find yourself" before choosing a career. Very few people graduate from institutes with a passion and a career path already laid out. With little or no experience in the business world how are you supposed to make the right career decisions that will impact the rest of your professional life? The answer: Proceed with caution and don't make hasty decisions - make educated decisions. Even if your parents are "well connected" and are friendly with many successful business people, chances are you won't have the opportunity to sit down with too many of them in- person and get some serious career advice

Once you have secured the interview, you should begin to focus on interview preparation. Do not be fooled into thinking that you can simply walk into an interview and answer a few questions. The employer will often meet with several hundred candidates in order to find 5-7 potential employees. Your goal must be to demonstrate your interest and qualifications for the position. Preparation is key!

Interviewers have many expectations of you as a candidate for potential hire. You must know general information about the position for which you are interviewing. You must also be able to articulate your qualifications and interest. In addition, the employer expects for you to have researched his/her organization and understand the nature of the organization. Many college seniors have not had the opportunity to participate in formal interviews; therefore the process may seem intimidating and complex. However, through research and practice, interviewing skills can be perfected. It is a widely known fact that the best candidate does not always get the job. Many qualified candidates are passed over due to lack of interview preparation or an inability to articulate "fit" for the position. Once you arrive at the interview stage, it is your ability to sell yourself that will help ensure a job offer.

Part of any effective job search includes preparing for that all-important interview, but are your interviewing skills up-to-date? What were considered correct responses in the 1990s could actually prevent you from getting a job these days. Why? Because the job climate has shifted and employers have different expectations of a prospective employee than they did even five years ago

Career : Don't Sabotage Your Job Search with False Assumptions
by Deborah Walker, CCMC

Most job seekers understand that the job market has changed radically over the last few years. Sadly, however, many still hold to job-search assumptions that do not apply to our current market conditions. If you believe any of the following five statements, you could be dragging your job search out longer than necessary. Cut your job search time by knowing the truth about the job market and learning how to combat these assumptions.

1. **"My last job search was a snap. I'm sure this time won't be any different."**

   Chances are, your last job search was in the mid to late 1990's when the job market favored job seekers. Even up to 2001, jobseekers (and even employers) lived under a rosy glow of unrealistic optimism. In the last few years, however, most job seekers have noticed a drastic drop in the market demand for their career skills. Persons who were once courted by recruiters and headhunters from top firms wonder why they are no longer receiving calls with enticing opportunities. For many job seekers, frustration and lack of confidence have replaced optimism.

   Action: The job seeker of 2004 will avoid discouragement by developing a strategic action plan that involves a high degree of proactive and systematic effort.

2. **"Employers and recruiters take the time to read entire resumes."**

   This is couldn't be farther from the truth. The reality is if the best information isn't in the top four to five inches of your resume, it's doubtful anyone will notice. Try this out for yourself. Open up your current resume on your computer. Do you see the entire first page? Probably not. Most likely when your resume is opened, the reader will see the top four to five inches. You must sell the reader in those first few inches or he/she is not going to bother scrolling down to read more. With the volume of resumes that employers and recruiters receive, who has the time to hunt out the good material on a resume?

Action : If your current resume isn't making best use of the top four to five inches, consider using a hybrid format that will allow you to place your best assets up on top where you'll be noticed and called.

3. **"I don't want to limit my potential job opportunities, so I'll write one resume to apply for all kinds of jobs."**

I learned early in my recruiting days that employers turn down perfectly qualified candidates because the resume's focus is too general. A one-size-fits-all resume gives the impression that the job seeker is uncertain of his career goal. An employer once told me that if a candidate is interested in two completely different positions, he must not be very good at either.

Action : The most effective resumes leave no doubt as to the job seeker's career objective. If you have more than one career objective, you need more than one resume.

4. **"I'm not going to bother with cover letters. No one really reads them anyway."** The truth is the quality of your cover letter often will determine whether your resume gets read at all. The worst offense, however, is to send a cover letter that sounds as "cookie-cutter" as junk mail.

Your cover letters will create a stronger first impression if you remember the buying motives of each of these major categories of recipients:

- Executive decision makers are most interested in your ability to help them achieve their corporate bottom-line objectives.
- HR screeners look for the best qualifications match.
- Third-party recruiters need strong selling points to help present you to their corporate clients.

Action : If you keep in mind the buying motives of your cover letter recipient, you'll win their attention more often than not.

5. **"If I can just get my foot in the door, my interview skills will get me an offer."**

   That may have been true back when you had less interview competition. But today, employers have the advantage of choosing from the best talent available, because so much of the best talent IS available. Since you'll probably be interviewing against candidates at least as strong as yourself, you'll need to distinguish yourself through superior interview preparation.

   Action : Remember that the best way to prepare for an interview is to think of an interview in three parts:
   - Ask questions to uncover the interviewer's hidden buying motives
   - Answer questions based on the interviewer's buying motives
   - Ask closing questions to win the job offer.

Interviewing is like being selected to compete in the Olympics: you have outperformed hundreds or thousands of competitors and are down to the final round. You are now competing with the best of the best. How can you leave with the gold? Here are keys to making your interview a day for the champion.

Analyze the Position

Before you are able to convince an employer that you want to be a Software trainee, it is important that you understand what a Software trainee does. To gather this important information, you may start with research in the Career Resource Library. Current resources such as the *Occupational Outlook Handbook*, provide up-to-date information regarding job responsibilities, employment outlook, educational requirements, and starting salaries. This basic research will prove valuable as you prepare to demonstrate a match between your credentials and the position for which you are interviewing.

In addition, you are encouraged to participate in an internship in a field you wish to pursue. An internship will help you gain experience and provide you with firsthand knowledge of the field. Informational interviews provide another excellent source of gathering information on specific career fields.

Organization Research

To begin, you must research the company or agency to determine the nature of the organization. The more that you know about the employer, the more comfortable you will feel in the interview. A demonstrated knowledge of the organization will also help convince the interviewer of your interest. In order to ascertain sincere interest, many interviewers will begin the process with a question such as, "Why are you interested in our organization?" or "Tell me what you know about our company." This is certainly not a question that you can "bluff" your way through. It is a mistake to assume you know enough about the organization without conducting any research. Only through research will you be able to answer the question with confidence. It is to your advantage to carefully research the job and the organization. There are many ways to do this. You can request printed materials from the employer, such as annual reports and job descriptions. This is an entirely appropriate request, so don't hesitate to make it. Use your library and career center resources. Ask colleagues, friends, and faculty about the organization, and about any personal contacts at the organization they might have. Look at the organization's home page. If you are interviewing with a privately held company or agency, you will need to be more creative in your research approach. If you cannot find information using the recommended methods, try identifying employees or volunteers (for nonprofit agencies) to gather information; the Chamber of Commerce may also be able to provide limited information. You may also consider talking with employees of similar organizations to gain a general perspective of the industry. Knowing about the job will help you prepare a list of your qualifications so that you can show, point by point, why you are the best candidate.

Through your research, you should become familiar with:
- Type of organization and its function
- Mission and goals
- Products or services
- Divisions and subsidiaries
- Position description and career paths
- Sales and earnings (if company is a public, for-profit organization)
- Size
- Competitors
- Location, including international operations (if applicable)
- Projects
- New trends in the field

Market Your Skills

After you have analyzed the position and researched the organization, you are now in a position to review your qualifications for the position. Knowing what you have to offer is crucial. Expressing yourself clearly and concisely is a key element of effective interviewing. Self-assessment of your skills, interests, and work values will help you organize your thoughts in order to project a positive impression.

A thorough self-assessment should enable you to:
- summarize your educational experiences as it relates to the position for which you are interviewing
- articulate your related skills and abilities
- cite examples of how you developed/used particular skills
- know your personal strengths and weaknesses
- discuss your work and cocurricular experiences in detail
- talk about your career goals and objectives
- know where you want to work
- identify any problem areas in your background and be prepared to discuss them
- discuss variables you are willing to negotiate (e.g. salary for geographical preference)

Making a Good First Impression

As cliche as it may sound, you will not get a second chance to make a first impression when it comes to interviews. Your nonverbal skills and the manner in which you present yourself will be evaluated in addition to your verbal responses to interview questions.

Be sure to arrive for your interview 10-15 minutes early. This will provide you with time to check your appearance and collect your thoughts prior to the interview. Be sure to greet the receptionist, secretary or others in the office in a friendly and courteous manner. These employees often have some influence in the hiring process.

As you are waiting on the interviewer to greet you, be sure to position yourself so that you have a good view of the hall or reception area from which you expect the employer to enter. You do not want to have your back facing the employer when he/she enters the room. When the employer greets you, be sure to stand and offer a firm handshake. Look the employer in the eyes and offer a return greeting similar to, "Nice to meet you." If the employer mispronounces your name, clearly state your name as you shake his/her hand. The only thing that you should be carrying is a portfolio with paper and pen; leave your coat and book bag (if you are interviewing on campus) in the waiting area unless otherwise instructed. You are always encouraged to take an extra copy of your resume with you for all interviews. For on-site interviews, women may also carry a small, professional looking purse.

As you enter the interview room, wait for the employer to indicate where you should be seated. After the employer is seated, it is your cue to also take a seat. During the interview, remember to practice good nonverbal skills:

- **Sit up straight with your shoulders back and hands resting in your lap**
- **Place both feet on the floor**
- **Maintain eye contact to demonstrate interest and enthusiasm**
- **Use limited hand gestures to emphasize key points**
- **Be aware of nervous movements such as tapping of your foot or playing with a ring**
- **Try to smile when responding to questions (when appropriate); a smile will indicate confidence and enthusiasm**
- **Try to relax; you will find that you are better able to respond to questions if you simply relax a little.**

Interview Attire

The way in which you dress for your interview will tell the employer about your professional savvy and, in some cases, will be one of the factors an employer will take into account in evaluating you as a candidate. Your ability to "dress the part" speaks to your knowledge of the industry and interest in "fitting in". Also, by dressing professionally, you will appear more mature and seasoned; this will aid you as you may be competing with older individuals with more experience. Understand that you will probably dress more professionally for an interview than may be required once you begin working in that environment. Appropriate interview attire will vary by field, however, you are best advised to dress professionally using the following guidelines from UCLA's 1999 Business Attire Survey:

Men and Women
- Two-piece business suit (navy or other dark color) / Sari
- Consistent look: avoid wearing a business suit with sandals or sneakers
- Well-groomed hair: avoid unusual styles or colors

- Minimal cologne or perfume
- No visible body art: cover tattoos with clothing if possible
- Breath mints; use one before greeting the recruiter
- No visible body piercings (other than earrings for women)

Women

- White, off-white, or neutral-colored blouse with a conservative neckline
- Suit with a skirt preferable to a pantsuit
- No ill-fitting (short, tight, clingy, or slit) skirts
- Closed-toe leather pumps with low to medium heels. Avoid open-toe strappy high heels, sandals, or shoes with decorations
- Skin-colored hosiery
- Briefcase or portfolio in place of a handbag or purse
- Conservative nail polish, avoid unusual colors, e.g., blue or green
- Understated makeup
- Small stud earrings instead of dangling or oversized earrings
- Long hair pulled back in a neat, simple style. No "big hair" or elaborate styles

Men

- Long-sleeved oxford cloth shirt in white or light blue
- Conservative necktie in terms of color and pattern. Avoid cartoon characters, less-than-serious graphics, or theme ties
- High-fitting dark socks. Avoid light colored socks with a dark suit
- Business-style leather shoes
- Matching shoe and belt color. Do not mix black and brown.
- Briefcase or portfolio, no backpack

Interview Tips

- Shake hands firmly.
- Look the employer in the eye when you are talking.
- Speak clearly, don't mumble.
- If you need time to think before answering, take time. Stick to the subject at hand, which is the job and your skills related to it.
- Use the employer's name, pronounce it correctly.

- Don't fidget in your seat and otherwise show nervousness with your body (hands, posture, etc.).
- Don't take notes during the interview if you can help it.
- Don't complain about a former boss or co-worker. By complaining in this way, you're likely to make the employer think that you are hard to get along with.
- Don't ask about salaries, sick leaves, pensions, vacations, or benefits in the first interview.
- Don't exaggerate; state the facts.
- If you have specific qualifications for a job, be sure the employer knows about them. No one knows what you can do unless you tell him or her.
- Talk about school subjects and hobbies that you have done well in and which are related to the job for which you are applying.
- An employer may be interested in everything you can do, but will be most interested in your skills that relate to the job for which you are applying.
- Ask questions when you don't understand what the employer is talking about. You'll want to know as much about the job as you can and asking questions is the best way to find out.
- The interviewer will close when he or she has enough information. Don't try to extend the interview unless you have an important point which has not been covered. Make it brief.
- Before leaving the interview (assuming you want the position), let the employer know that you really want the job. By doing this, the employer will feel that you will work hard and that you will want to stay on the job.

Communicate Effectively

Though it is imperative for you to know yourself and the organization with which you are interviewing, if you are unable to communicate your knowledge clearly and concisely, your interview will not be impressive. You must be able to express yourself to the interviewer.

The best way to improve your communication skills is to practice role-playing before the interview. Consider participating in a mock interview through the Career Center or ask a friend, your spouse, or roommate, to help simulate an interview. Make sure you are critiqued on the strength of your voice and eye contact.

Another suggestion for role-playing might be to get together with people who are also preparing for interviews. You could learn a lot by critiquing different approaches and this might also be a good way to boost each other's morale.

A critical point to remember while practicing, is to avoid memorizing what you want to say. Whether you are talking about yourself or the organization with which you are interviewing, let it be a natural flow of words. If you come across like you have a speech prepared, your interview will be less effective.

You probably will be nervous during the interview. Concentrate on what is being asked and respond appropriately. Many people make their voices more monotone to sound professional. Don't! Use normal tone and don't speak too softly.

The Interview Process

The first interview you will encounter is called a screening interview. It may take place on campus (through the On-campus Interview Program), at a job fair, or at the employer's office. This type of interview generally lasts 30 minutes to one hour. The purpose of the screening interview is to separate unqualified applicants from qualified ones. An invitation for a second interview may be offered in a few days from the screening interview or it may take up to four weeks. Usually, only a small percentage of candidates will be invited back for the second interview.

The second interview is an in-depth interview conducted at the site of the organization. It may last anywhere from one hour to two days. Some employers may even call you back three or four times before making a decision regarding your candidacy.

Through your research, you should be able to identify three to five skills that you believe the employer will seek in a successful candidate. With this in mind, carefully consider your background and qualifications. Be prepared to discuss examples of these skills by describing specific experiences and accomplishments from your past. Do not assume that the interviewer will appreciate your qualifications by reading your resume. It is up to you to demonstrate enthusiasm and "fit" for the position.

Having carefully prepared for this moment, you should approach the interview with confidence. Each interview will be different; some interviews will be very structured and formal while others may be casual and informal. Interviewing styles will vary. Do not become overly concerned if the person who is interviewing you asks difficult questions; try to remain calm and respond to all questions in a positive manner.

The interview generally consists of five interrelated stages: introduction and icebreaker; verifying information and asking questions; responding to your questions; closing the interview and decision-making.

The first stage is a basic introduction and "ice breaker".

The interviewer will try to establish rapport with you by talking about an unrelated topic such as the weather. Keep all of your comments positive, even if the weather is terrible that day; the employer will have concerns if you start off complaining about small, insignificant events.

After a few minutes of introduction, the employer will begin asking questions and verifying information from your resume. As each question is posed, take a moment to consider your answer. Try not to look up at the ceiling or down at the floor as you consider your reply. Start your response in a positive note; be careful not to start with "um" or another verbal filler. Be sure to provide specific examples of accomplishments to demonstrate skills.

A helpful outline for answering interview questions is best described through the S.T.A.R. (situation, task, action, and result) method. Using this method, you would respond to an interview question with an example of a situation or a task for which you were responsible. Thoroughly describe the actions that you took in this situation or task. Emphasize specific results or accomplishments. Remember that numbers can be impressive. Always speak in first person when describing the situation. Whenever possible, try to articulate the value of the experience in terms of how the experience has prepared you for the position for which you are interviewing. Do not be overly concerned if the interviewer is taking notes during the interview process. Keep your composure and try to keep your eyes level so that when the employer looks up, you will have eye contact.

The Second Interview

Very few employment offers are made after a screening interview. Before an offer is extended, an employer will generally require a second interview. Being invited for a second interview indicates that the employer has sincere interest in you as a candidate; however, it does not mean that a job offer is pending. Again, it is your responsibility to prepare for the interview and do your best to market your skills and abilities. Before accepting the invitation, carefully assess your interest in the organization. Only accept an invitation for a second interview if you have an interest in the organization.

A second interview may last from one hour to two full days; the most typical interviews last from four to six hours. If the interview is within driving distance, be sure to confirm directions and parking instructions. You may even want to drive to the location a day or two in advance to alleviate any logistical concerns; you don't want to get lost on your way to the interview and arrive late.

If your second interview necessitates long distance travel, a company representative will generally make airline and hotel arrangements for you. Be sure to ask this representative if other expenses, such as meals, will be prepaid or if you should plan on paying for these expenses and submitting receipts.

Before your interview, you should receive a schedule which includes the names and titles of the people with whom you will meet. If you do not receive a schedule, you should call and ask for this information. Be sure to know the name of the person for whom you should ask when you arrive on site. Plan to arrive 15 minutes early so you can check your appearance and collect your thoughts prior to the start of your interviews. As always, politely greet the receptionist or others you may meet while waiting on your interview.

Throughout the course of the day, you may meet with a number of different employees. Pay close attention to their names and titles. A title may help you understand the type of response that particular individual is seeking. For example, if the interviewer is a manager, he/she may be looking at work ethic as well as general knowledge; if the interviewer is a potential colleague, he/she may be looking for someone who is a team player; if the interviewer is the financial manager of the organization, his/her questions will probably center on your knowledge and experience in budgeting and finance.

You should prepare for the second interview just as you prepared for the screening interview: thoroughly review your research on the organization, gathering additional information if possible, and be prepared to demonstrate a match between your qualifications and the position. Good communication skills are very important at this stage.

Salary

One question you should be ready to answer is on the salary expected. On your resume it is proper not to mention salaries. You can even leave it open on your application form or write in negotiable. But in an interview, you might be asked to state a figure. Know what persons of your general qualifications are being offered as starting salaries in positions similar to the one for which you are interviewing. For salary information, consult resources in the Career Library. There are also a variety of Web sites that provide salary information. Examples include www.salary.com, hotjobs.yahoo.com/salary and salary.monster.com. Many other sites can be found by simply searching the Web using the term "salary." These sources can give you some idea of what your salary range will be. By knowing the rate beforehand, you can be realistic in your terms. Candidates whose rates are too high might price themselves right out of the job. If you are too low, the interviewer might not consider you an ambitious person, and there is a chance you will not be given further consideration. Another possibility is that they might hire you at a lower rate and there will be no chance for negotiating a salary figure. One way to handle salary questions is to give a salary range. Be prepared to back up your salary request with specific information about your education and experience. Generally however, it is recommended that candidates allow employers to address salary.

If You Have the Right Skills, Does it Matter if Your Tongue is Pierced?
Can a tattoo trash your chance at a job with some employers? Will a purple streak in your hair push you out of the running as a job candidate? Are piercings prohibited in the real "world of work"?
Employers who responded to the *Job Outlook 2006* survey say a job candidate's grooming has a strong influence on their opinion of the candidate. (See Figure) The two things most likely to influence an employer? Personal grooming (Do you have body odor or smell too strongly of cologne? Are your face and hands clean?) and interview attire (Business attire vs. jeans and a T-shirt) clean and unwrinkled. Employers reviewed a list of possible physical attributes and rated each on how it would influence their opinions of a candidate's suitability for employment and how much. "These results are consistent with what we've seen in the past," says Marilyn Mackes, executive director of the National Association of Colleges and Employers, the nonprofit organization that conducts the Job Outlook survey. "Job candidates need to remember that their overall grooming and choice of interview attire project an image; they are marketing themselves to the employer as a potential employee, and part of marketing is the packaging."

Interestingly, employers indicated that a candidate's handshake is likely to have a greater influence on their opinion of a candidate than many other more obvious attributes, such as unusual hairstyles and colors, tattoos, and body piercings. However, that doesn't give job candidates license to dye, tattoo, or pierce with abandon, cautions Mackes.

"It's important for job seekers to recognize that attributes that exert even a slight influence over an employer can be just as important as those that exert a strong influence," says Mackes. "When an employer has to make a choice among job candidates, these are the items that could make or break a candidacy."

Best advice? Be conservative.

Attribute	No Influence	Slight Influence	Strong Influence
Grooming	6%	21%	73%
Nontraditional interview attire	13%	38%	49%
Handshake	22%	45%	33%
Body piercing	26%	43%	31%
Obvious tattoos	25%	46%	29%
Nontraditional hair colour	26%	46%	28%
Unusual hairstyle	30%	49%	21%
Earring (male)	54%	34%	12%
Beard	73%	22%	5%
Mustache	83%	16%	1%

Figure 1: Candidate physical attributes and their influence on employers, by percent of respondents

Career development and job-search advice for new college graduates.

How College Students Can Avoid Getting "Whittled Out"

In a struggling economy, hiring managers get flooded with resumes for job openings. How can you avoid being whittled out of the candidate mix in the early stages? In a recent *Newsday* article, hiring managers had several suggestions for job seekers. In addition, NACE's 2003 *Planning Job Choices* provided resume tips for new graduates from employers, career counselors, and recent graduates.

Tips from these sources include:

Pay attention to detail—You probably have sent out dozens of resumes and may be tempted to cut corners by, for instance, by not proofreading your cover letter, failing to include information the hiring manager asked for, or beginning a cover letter "Dear Sir or Madam" when the hiring manager's name is on the company web site. The moral to this story? Take the time to make sure the correspondence and information you send is correct and error-free.

Do the basics—Proofread for spelling, grammar, and tone, and make sure you have followed the instructions of the employer. Firing off an e-mail is a convenient method of communication. However, don't let the sloppy nature and informality of e-mail correspondence seep into your communications—whether it's e-mailed or written—with potential employers.

Construct an effective resume—Organize the information in a logical fashion and keep descriptions clear and to the point. Include as much work experience as possible, even if it obviously doesn't relate to the job you are seeking. Also, use a simple, easy-to-read font.

Customize your response—Address the hiring manager directly, and include the name of the company and the position for which it is hiring in your cover letter/e-mail response.

Make it easy for the hiring manager—Use your name and the word "resume" in the e-mail header so it's easy to identify. If the employer asks for information—such as references or writing samples—make sure to provide it.

Focus on what you take to the employer, not what you want from the job—This is an opportunity for you to market yourself and stand out from the other candidates. What can you do to make the hiring manager's life easier? What can you do to help the company?

Be professional—You won't be taken seriously if they don't have e-mail or voice mail/answering machine. If you don't have e-mail, for instance, free accounts are available through Yahoo! and Hotmail. Provide the recruiter with a cell phone number if your voice mail/answering machine doesn't pick up when you are online. Also, it's a good idea for you to ditch the cute e-mail address or voice mail/answering machine messages in favor of ones that are more professional.

Any fact facing us is not as important as our attitude toward it,
for that determines our success or failure."
- Norman Vincent Peale -

Interviewing-What is it?
- A structured meeting between you and an employer, Interviewing is a skill- like riding your bike
- PRACTICE makes PERFECT

Interviewing is a two-way street
- Employers are attempting to determine if you are an appropriate fit for the job and their culture.
- You decide if the environment is right for you.

Types of Interviews
- **Phone :** used as an initial screen of candidates or to narrow the pool of applicants
- **One-on-One:** most common interview style and incorporates you with the potential employer
- **Panel or Group:** allows many individuals to interview you at once
- **Meal:** used to see how you interact or function in a social setting
- **Second or On-site Interview**: this allows one to get a tour of the facility, meet the staff, and additional questioning from different employees and/or administration

Pre-Interview Preparation
- Research position, company, & industry
- Know yourself and be able to articulate skills, strengths, accomplishments, and career goals
- Prepare necessary materials (Copies of resume, references, portfolio/pen, palm pilot or organizer.
- Ask for directions and where to park
- Be sure to allow yourself plenty of time to arrive at your destination

Greeting & Introduction
- Only 1 chance to make a good 1st impression
- Dress appropriately
- Smile
- Maintain eye contact
- Firm handshake
- Remain poised and confident

Interpersonal Skills
- Pleasant and polite manner
- Friendly and interested
- Acceptant and non-judgemental attitude
- Willingness to listen
- Empathy
- Maintain control of interview
- Probe gently but incisively
- Present a measure of experience and authority

Body Language

What signals are you sending?

Positive Signals
- Leaning forward = interest
- Smiling = friendly
- Nodding = attentive and alert
- Eye contact = curious and focused

Negative Signals
- Crossed arms = defensive
- Fidgeting hands or tapping feet = nervous or bored
- Lack of eye contact = untrustworthy
- Leaning back = discomfort

Components of the Interview
- Opening
- Information gathering
- Information giving
- Closing
- Evaluating

Research The Company

Know the following:
- How old the company is
- What its products or services are
- Where its plants, offices or stores are located

- What its growth has been
- How its prospects look for the future

Types of Interview Questions

A. Standard or traditional-

Targeting your education, work experiences, and career goals.

Sample Questions
- Tell me about yourself?
- What is your greatest strength? Weakness?
- Why did you choose to interview with us?
- What did you like most about your last job? Least?
- What are your short and long term career goals?

B. Behavioral Questions
- These focus on your actions and/or behaviors in a previous setting.
- Past behavior provides clues to future behavior

Sample Questions
- Describe a time you had to make a difficult decision?
- Tell me about a time you worked under a deadline?
- What do you do when a team member is not pulling his/her weight?
- Think about a time you made a mistake. What did you learn from it?

C. Inappropriate or unethical questions
- Questions which probe into your private life or personal background
- Questions about your ethnicity, religion, sexual orientation, disabilities, marital status

Sample Questions
- How old are you?
- Do you have children?
- Do you have a disability?
- What religion do you practice?

D. Questions asked by the interviewee

To determine if you are an appropriate fit for the company and position, prepare a list of questions for the interviewer

Sample Questions
- What type of assignments can I expect within the first year?
- What do you like most about this company?
- What is the biggest challenge facing this department right now?
- What skills are you looking for in this position?
- What is the next course of action?

General Interview Strategies
- Be prepared to talk about yourself and your experiences
- Master the art of storytelling
- Provide specific and concrete examples of your results/accomplishments
- Remain positive, enthusiastic, poised, and confident throughout the interview process.
- Remember an interview is a formal conversation—avoid filler words like "Um", "Ah", & "You know"
- Avoid indecisive phrases like: "I think," "I guess," "probably," or "pretty good"
- Think before speaking
- Avoid long verbose answers—limit your response to 1-2 minutes
- If you do not hear or understand a question, ask them to clarify it for you.
- Remain calm, relaxed, and be yourself
- Try to focus on the message you are trying to convey—NOT how well you are doing

FOLLOW-UP
- Ask good questions
- Thank the interviewer
- Request a business card
- Inquire about next steps in the process

SUGGESTIONS
- Conduct a test run the day before the interview
- Practice! Practice! Practice!

- Obtain a list of practice interview questions and jot down short answers
- Stand in front of a mirror and rehearse your answers
- Schedule an appointment for a mock interview with Career Services
- Get a good night's sleep–be well rested and alert for the interview
- Be relaxed and be yourself!

VERBAL AND NON-VERBAL MESSAGES

Not all of what you get across to an employer in an interview is through the answers you give to questions. In fact, only 7% of your impact is through words. The chart above shows the impact that your "non-verbal messages" (tonality and body language) make on an interviewer

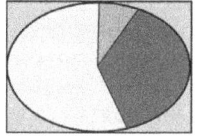

WHAT ARE EMPLOYERS LOOKING FOR?
- Communication Skills
- Team Building Abilities
- Leadership Skills
- Creativity
- Problem Solving Skills
- Coping Skills/Adaptability/Self Control
- Decisiveness (can you make a decision?)
- Initiative/Motivation
- Ability to Juggle Multiple Tasks
- Commitment to Completing Tasks
- Organizational and Planning Skills
- Current Technical Abilities
- Quality

Interview Do's and Don'ts

To Do's — Arrive 15 minutes early. Late attendance is never excusable. Clarify questions. Be sure you answered the questions the employer really asked. Get the interviewer to describe the position and responsibilities early in the conversation so you can relate your skills and background to the position throughout the interview. Give your qualifications. Stress the accomplishments that are most pertinent to the job. Conduct yourself professionally. Be aware of what your body language is saying. Smile, make eye contact, don't slouch and maintain composure. Anticipate tough questions. Prepare in advance so you can turn apparent weaknesses into strengths. Dress appropriately. Make your first impression a professional one. Ask questions throughout the interview. An interview should be a mutual exchange of information, not a one-sided conversation. Listen. This is probably the most important "do" of all. By concentrating not only on the employer's words, but also on the tone of voice and body language, you will be able to pick up on the employer's style. Once you understand how a hiring authority thinks, pattern your answers accordingly and you will be able to better relate to him or her.

Not To Do's —Don't answer vague questions. Rather than answering questions you think you hear, get the employer to be more specific and then respond. Never interrupt the employer. If you don't have time to listen, neither does the employer. Don't smoke, chew gum or place anything on the employer's desk. Don't be overly familiar, even if the employer is doing all of these things. Don't wear heavy perfume or cologne. Don't ramble. Long answers often make the speaker sound apologetic or indecisive. On the other hand, don't answer questions with a simple "yes" or "no." Explain whenever possible. Do not lie. Answer questions as truthfully as possible. Do not make derogatory remarks about your present or former employers or companies.

Too many people second-guess themselves after an interview. By closing strongly and asking the right questions, you can eliminate the post-interview doubts that tend to plague most interviewees. If you feel that the interview went well and you would like to take the next step, express your interest to the hiring authority and turn the tables a bit. Try something like the following:

"After hearing more about your company, the position and the responsibilities at hand, I am certain that I possess the qualities that you are looking for in the (title) position. Based on our conversation and my qualifications, are there any issues or concerns that you have that would lead you to believe otherwise?"

You have a right to be assertive. This is a great closing question because it opens the door for the hiring authority to be honest with you about his or her feelings. If concerns do exist, this is a great opportunity to overcome them. You have one final chance to dispel the concerns, sell your strengths and end the interview on positive note.

A few things to remember during the closing process: Don't be discouraged if no definite offer is made or specific salary discussed. The interviewer will probably want to communicate with the office first, or interview other applicants, before making a decision.

Make sure you answer the following two questions: "why are you interested in the company?," and "what can you offer?" Express thanks for the interviewer's time and consideration. Ask for their business card so you can write a thank you letter as soon as possible.

When you get in your car, immediately write down key issues uncovered during the interview. Think of the qualifications the employer is looking for and match your strengths to them. This follow-up processes is very critical. A "thank you" letter should be written no later than 24 hours after the interview.

After The Interview

Write A Follow-up Letter Ask for the interviewer's business card and write him/her a letter or follow-up e-mail. But make it more than a plain thank-you note. Tell him/her you are still interested in the position and go over some of your qualifications that were discussed in the interview so that his/her memory will be refreshed. Possibly include a couple of pertinent questions that you did not ask in the interview. If s/he answers you quickly, this might be an indication that s/he is interested in you.

COMMON INTERVIEW QUESTIONS AND ANSWERS (HR)

Interviews are always stressful - even for job seekers who have gone on countless interviews. The best way to reduce the stress is to be prepared. Take the time to review the "standard" interview questions you will most likely be asked. Review these typical interview questions and think about how you would answer them. Read the questions listed; you will also find some strategy suggestions with it.

1. *Tell me about yourself?*

    The most often asked question in interviews. You need to have a short statement prepared in your mind. Be careful that it does not sound rehearsed. Limit it to work related items unless instructed otherwise. Talk about things you have done and jobs you have held that relate to the position you are interviewing for. Start with the item farthest back and work up to the present.

2. *Why did you leave your last job?*

    Stay positive regardless of the circumstances. Never refer to a major problem with management and never speak ill of supervisors, co-workers or the organization. If you do, you will be the one looking bad. Keep smiling and talk about leaving for a positive reason such as an opportunity, a chance to do something special or other forward-looking reasons.

3. *What experience do you have in this field?*

    Speak about specifics that relate to the position you are applying for. If you do not have specific experience, get as close as you can.

4. *Do you consider yourself successful?*

    You should always answer yes and briefly explain why. A good explanation is that you have set goals, and you have met some and are on track to achieve the others.

5. *What do co-workers say about you?*

    Be prepared with a quote or two from co-workers. Either a specific statement or a paraphrase will work. Jill Clark, a co-worker at Smith Company, always said I was the hardest workers she had ever known. It is as powerful as Jill having said it at the interview herself.

6. *What do you know about this organization?*

    This question is one reason to do some research on the organization before the interview. Find out where they have been and where they are going. What are the current issues and who are the major players?

7. *What have you done to improve your knowledge in the last year?*

    Try to include improvement activities that relate to the job. A wide variety of activities can be mentioned as positive self-improvement. Have some good ones handy to mention.

8. *Are you applying for other jobs?*

    Be honest but do not spend a lot of time in this area. Keep the focus on this job and what you can do for this organization. Anything else is a distraction.

9. *Why do you want to work for this organization?*

    This may take some thought and certainly, should be based on the research you have done on the organization. Sincerity is extremely important here and will easily be sensed. Relate it to your long-term career goals.

10. *Do you know anyone who works for us?*

    Be aware of the policy on relatives working for the organization. This can *affect* your answer even though they asked about friends not relatives. Be careful to mention a friend only if they are well thought of.

11. **What kind of salary do you need?**

    A loaded question. A nasty little game that you will probably lose if you answer first. So, do not answer it. Instead, say something like, That's a tough question. Can you tell me the range for this position? In most cases, the interviewer, taken *off* guard, will tell you. If not, say that it can depend on the details of the job. Then give a wide range.

12. **Are you a team player?**

    You are, of course, a team player. Be sure to have examples ready. Specifics that show you often perform for the good of the team rather than for yourself are good evidence of your team attitude. Do not brag, just say it in a matter-of-fact tone. This is a key point.

13. **How long would *you* expect to work for us if hired?**

    Specifics here are not good. Something like this should work: I'd like it to be a long time. Or As long as we both feel I'm doing a good job.

14. **Have you ever had to fire anyone? How did you feel about that?**

    This is serious. Do not make light of it or in any way seem like you like to fire people. At the same time, you will do it when it is the right thing to do. When it comes to the organization versus the individual who has created a harmful situation, you will protect the organization. Remember firing is not the same as loyoff or reduction in force

15. **What is your philosophy towards work?**

    The interviewer is not looking for a long or flowery dissertation here. Do you have strong feelings that the job gets done? Yes. That's the type of answer that works best here. Short and positive, showing a benefit to the organization.

16. **If you had enough money to retire right now, would you?**

    Answer yes if you would. But since you need to work, this is the type of work you prefer. Do not say yes if you do not mean it.

17. **Have you ever been asked to leave a position?**

    If you have not, say no. If you have, be honest, brief and avoid saying negative things about the people or organization involved.

18. **Explain how you would be an asset to this organization**

    You should be anxious for this question. It gives you a chance to highlight your best points as they relate to the position being discussed. Give a little advance thought to this relationship.

19. **Why should we hire you?**

    Point out how your assets meet what the organization needs. Do not mention any other candidates to make a comparison.

20. **Tell me about a suggestion you have made**

    Have a good one ready. Be sure and use a suggestion that was accepted and was then considered successful. One related to the type of work applied for is a real plus.

21. **What irritates you about co-workers?**

    This is a trap question. Think real hard but fail to come up with anything that irritates you. A short statement that you seem to get along with folks is great.

22. **What is your greatest strength?**

    Numerous answers are good, just stay positive. A few good examples:

    Your ability to prioritize, Your problem-solving skills, Your ability to work under pressure, Your ability to focus on projects, Your professional expertise, Your leadership skills, Your positive attitude.

23. **Tell me about your dream job.**

    Stay away from a specific job. You cannot win. If you say the job you are contending for is it, you strain credibility. If you say another job is it, you plant the suspicion that you will be dissatisfied with this position if hired. The best is to stay genetic and say something like: A job where I love the work, like the people, can contribute and can't wait to get to work.

24. **Why do you think you would do well at this job?**

    Give several reasons and include skills, experience and interest.

25. **What are you looking for In a job?** See answer # 23
26. **What kind of person would you refuse to work with?**

    Do not be trivial. It would take disloyalty to the organization, violence or lawbreaking to get you to object. Minor objections will label you as a winner.

27. **What is more important to you: the money or the work?**

    Money is always important, but the work is the most important. There is no better answer.

28. **What would your previous supervisor say your strongest point is?**

    There are numerous good possibilities:

    Loyalty, Energy, Positive attitude, Leadership, Team player, Expertise, Initiative, Patience, Hard work, Creativity, Problem solver

29. **Tell me about a problem you had with a supervisor**

    Biggest trap of all. This is a test to see if you will speak ill of your boss. If you fall for it and tell about a problem with a former boss, you may well below the interview right there. Stay positive and develop a poor memory about any trouble with a supervisor.

30. **What has disappointed you about a job?**

    Don't get trivial or negative. Safe areas are few but can include:

    Not enough of a challenge. You were laid off in a reduction Company did not win a contract, which would have given you more responsibility.

31. **Tell me about your ability to work under pressure.**

    You may say that you thrive under certain types of pressure. Give an example that relates to the type of position applied for.

32. **Do your skills match this job or another job more closely?**

    Probably this one. Do not give fuel to the suspicion that you may want another job more than this one.

33. **What motivates you to do your best on the job?**

    This is a personal trait that only you can say, but good examples are: Challenge, Achievement,

34. **Are you willing to work overtime? Nights? Weekends?**

    This is up to you. Be totally honest.

35. **How would you know you were successful on this job?**

    Several ways are good measures : You set high standards for yourself and meet them. Your outcomes are a success. Your boss tell you that you are successful

36. **Would you be willing to relocate if required?**

    You should be clear on this with your family prior to the interview if you think there is a chance it may come up. Do not say yes just to get the job if the real answer is no. This can create a lot of problems later on in your career. Be honest at this point and save yourself future grief.

37. **Are you willing to put the interests of the organization ahead of your own?**

    This is a straight loyalty and dedication question. Do not worry about the deep ethical and philosophical implications. Just say yes.

38. **Describe your management style.**

    Try to avoid labels. Some of the more common labels, like progressive, salesman or consensus, can have several meanings or descriptions depending on which management expert you listen to. The situational style is safe, because it says you will manage according to the situation, instead of one size fits all.

39. **What have you learned from mistakes on the job?**

    Here you have to come up with something or you strain credibility. Make it small, well intentioned mistake with a positive lesson learned. An example would be working too far ahead of colleagues on a project and thus throwing coordination off.

40. **Do you have any blind spots?**

    Trick question. If you know about blind spots, they are no longer blind spots. Do not reveal any personal areas of concern here. Let them do their own discovery on your bad points. Do not hand it to them.

41. **If you were hiring a person for this job, what would you look for?**

    Be careful to mention traits that are needed and that you have.

42. **Do you think you are overqualified for this position?**

    Regardless of your qualifications, state that you are very well qualified for the position.

43. **How do you propose to compensate for your lack of experience?**

    First, if you have experience that the interviewer does not know about, bring that up: Then, point out (if true) that you are a hard working quick learner.

44. **What qualities do you look for in a boss?**

    Be generic and positive. Safe qualities are knowledgeable, a sense of humor, fair, loyal to subordinates and holder of high standards. All bosses think they have these traits.

45. **Tell me about a time when you helped resolve a dispute between others.**

    Pick a specific incident. Concentrate on your problem solving technique and not the dispute you settled.

46. **What position do you prefer on a team working on a project?**

    'Be honest. If you are comfortable in different roles, point that out.

47. **Describe your work ethic.**

    Emphasize benefits to the organization. Things like, determination to get the job done and work hard but enjoy your work.

48. **What has been your biggest professional disappointment?**

    Be sure that you refer to something that was beyond your control. Show acceptance and no negative feelings.

49. **Tell me about the most fun you have had on the job.**

    Talk about having fun by accomplishing something for the organization.

50. **Do you have any questions for me?**

    Always have some questions prepared. Questions prepared where you will be an asset to the organization are good. How soon will I be able to be productive? and What type of projects will I be able to assist on? Are some examples.

Group Discussion

Group discussion: Winners' skills

Group discussion is an important dimension of the job selection process. Any job requires employees to work with others for effective functioning. Therefore, people skills are an important aspect of any job. In today's context, the organizations are interested in team players rather than individual contributors even if they are excellent performers by themselves.

Employers during group discussion evaluate the candidates' potential to be a leader and also his/her ability to work in teams.

Normally group discussions are used in the selection process for management trainees and executive positions. Employers are looking for candidates **who have potential to be executives and to lead teams of people.**

Here's how most group discussions work

Normally groups of 8-10 candidates are formed into a leaderless group, and are given a specific situation to analyze and discuss within a given time limit.

They may be given a case study and asked to come out with a solution for a problem.

They may be given a topic and are asked to discuss on the same.

A panel, which normally comprises the functional and HR executives of the company will observe and evaluate the members of the group.

Here is a sample list of skills assessed during a group discussion process:

Leadership skills

Ability to take leadership roles and be able to lead, inspire and carry the team along to help them achieve group's objectives.

Example : *To be able to initiate the group discussion, or be able to guide the group especially when the discussion begins losing relevance or try to encourage all members to participate in the discussion.*

Communication skills

The participating candidates will be assessed in terms of clarity of thought, expression and aptness of language. One key aspect is listening. It indicates a willingness to accommodate others views.

Example : *To be able to use simple language and explain concepts clearly so that it is easily understood by all.*

Interpersonal skills

Is reflected in the ability of the individual to interact with other members of the group in a brief situation. Emotional maturity and balance promotes good interpersonal relationships. The person has to be more people centric and less self-centered.

Example : To remain cool even when someone provokes you by with personal comment, ability to remain objective, ability to empathize, non-threatening and more of a team player.

Persuasive skills

In terms of ability to analyse and persuade others to see the problem from multiple perspectives without hurting the group members.

Example : While appreciating the other person's point of view, should be able to effectively communicate your view without obviously contradicting the other person's opinions.

Problem solving skills

Ability to come out with divergent and offbeat solutions and uses one's own creativity.

Example : While thinking of solutions, don't be afraid to think of novel solutions. This is a high- risk high-return strategy.

Conceptualizing skills :

The ability to grasp the situation, take it from the day to day mundane problem level and apply it to a macro level.

Example: At the end of the discussion, you could probably summarize the findings in a few sentences that present the overall perspective.

A note of caution – Can we acquire all the skills overnight or can we put up a show?

A group discussion is a simulated exercise, where you cannot suddenly put up a show, since the evaluators will see through you easily.

"Group discussion allows you to exchange information and ideas and gives you the experience of working in a team. In the work place, discussions enable management to draw on the ideas and expertise of staff, and to acknowledge the staff as valued members of a team

Why Have a Discussion?
- It helps you to understand a subject or topic area more deeply.
- It expands and clarifies your knowledge.
- It improves your ability to think critically.
- It helps a group to make a particular decision or come to a conclusion.
- It gives you the chance to hear the thoughts and ideas of other students.
- It improves your language skills.
- It increases your confidence in speaking.
- It can change your attitudes and ideas.

What can I get out of group discussion?
- Ideas can be generated.
- Ideas can be shared.
- Ideas can be 'tried out'.
- Ideas can be responded to by others.

- When the dynamics are right, groups provide a supportive and nurturing environment for academic and professional Endeavor.
- Group discussion skills have many professional applications.
- Working in groups is fun!

During an effective group discussion each participant may take up a number of task and maintenance to keep the discussion moving productively.

As well as these positive roles like Initiator, Information seeker, Information giver, Procedure facilitator, Opinion seeker, Opinion giver, Clarifier, Summarizer, there are a number of negative roles like Disgruntled non-participant, Attacker, Dominator, Clown, which are often taken up in group discussion. You should avoid taking up these roles and learn to identify them in other group members.

1. *Team Player :* Initiating the discussion, however, consistent quality of contributions is preferable to the "Started with a bang and ended with a whimper" approach.
2. *Reasoning Ability :* Reasoning ability plays an important role while expressing your opinions or ideas at a GD
3. *Leadership :* A GD where participants are unable to establish a proper rapport and do not speak much.
    ~ A GD where participants get emotionally charged and the GD gets chaotic.
    ~ A GD where participants discuss the topic assertively by touching on all its nuances and try to reach the objective.

Here, a leader would be someone who facilitates the third situation at a GD.

A leader would have the following qualities:
~ S/he shows direction to the group whenever group moves away from the topic.
~ S/he coordinates the effort of the different team members in the GD.
~ S/he contributes to the GD at regular intervals with valuable insights.
~ S/he also inspires and motivates team members to express their views.

4. *Flexibility* :
    - You must be open to other ideas as well as to the evaluation of your ideas:
    - But first, remember: Never ever start your GD with a stand or a conclusion.

- Say the topic of a GD is, 'Should India go to war with Pakistan?'
- Some participants tend to get emotionally attached to the topic and take a stand either in favour or against the topic, ie 'Yes, India should', or, 'No, India should not'.
- By taking a stand, you have already given your decision without discussing the topic at hand or listening to the views of your team members.
- Also, if you encounter an opposition with a very strong point at the 11th hour, you end up in a typical catch-22 situation:
- If you change your stand, you are seen as a fickle-minded or a whimsical person.

5. *Assertiveness*
   - You must put forth your point to the group in a very emphatic, positive and confident manner.
   - Participants often confuse assertiveness with aggressiveness

6. *Initiative*
   - A general trend amongst students is to start a GD and get the initial kitty of points earmarked for the initiator.
   - But that is a high risk-high return strategy.
   - Initiate a GD only if you are well versed with the topic. If you start and fail to contribute at regular intervals, it gives the impression that you started the GD just for the sake of the initial points.

7. *Creativity*

   An idea or a perspective which opens new horizons for discussion on the GD topic is always highly appreciated

8. **Inspiring ability**

   A good group discussion should incorporate views of all the team members.
   - If some team members want to express their ideas but are not getting the opportunity to do so, giving them an opportunity to express their ideas or opinions will be seen as a positive trait.
   - *Caution :* If a participant is not willing to speak, you need not necessarily go out of the way to ask him to express his views. This may insult him and hamper the flow of the GD.

9. *Listening*

   Always try and strike a proper balance between expressing your ideas and imbibing ideas

   Don't use redundant transition words like, In my opinion...

Communication Skill 125

Discussion Etiquette (*or minding your manners*)
In order to successfully negotiate discussion, courtesy is important.

The following are a few ground rules for good conduct

Do

- Respect the contribution of other speakers. Speak clearly
- Speak pleasantly and with courtesy to all members of the group.
- Listen well to the ideas of other speakers; you will learn something.
- Remember that a discussion is not a fight. Learn to disagree politely.
- Respect that others have differing views and are not neccessarily 'wrong'.
- Think about your contribution before you speak. How best can you answer the question/ contribute to the topic?
- Try to stick to the discussion topic. Don't introduce irrelevant information.
- Be aware of your body language when you are speaking. Keep it 'open' and friendly. Avoid gestures that appear aggressive.
- Agree with and acknowledge what you find interesting.
- Stay with the topic. If the discussion does digress, bring it back on topic by saying something like 'Just a final point about the last topic before we move on' or 'that's an interesting point, can we come back to that later?

Don't

- Don't take offence if a person disagrees with you. There will be times when other speakers will have different points of view. They may disagree with your ideas, and they are entitled to do so.
- Don't ridicule the contribution of others. Don't use comments like 'that's stupid', that's ridiculous, or 'you're wrong'.
- Don't try to intimidate or insult another speaker.
- Don't use a loud or angry tone. Others will not want to listen to you if you are being aggressive. Use a moderate tone and medium pitch.
- Avoid negative body language when speaking. Gestures like finger-pointing and table-thumping appear aggressive.
- Try not to dominate the discussion. Confident speakers should allow quieter students a chance to contribute.
- Avoid drawing too much on personal experience or anecdote. Although some tutors encourage students to reflect on their own experience, remember not to generalise too much.

Many companies conduct group discussion after the written test so as to check on your interactive skills and how good you are at communicating with other people. The GD is to check how you behave, participate and contribute in a group, how much importance do you give to the group objective as well as your own, how well do you listen to viewpoints of others and how open-minded are you in accepting views contrary to your own. The aspects which make up a GD are verbal communication, non-verbal behaviour, conformation to norms, decision-making ability and cooperation

Strategies for Improving Your Discussion Skills

Asking questions and joining in discussions are important skills for university study. In many subjects, you will receive marks for 'tutorial participation', and this mark reflects how active you have been in tutorial discussions. So, aim to speak at least once in each discussion.

If you find it difficult to speak or ask questions in tutorials, try the following strategies.

Observe

Attend as many seminars and tutorials as possible and notice what other students do. Ask yourself:

- **How do other students make critical comments?**
- **How do they ask questions?**
- **How do they disagree with or support the topic?**
- **What special phrases do they use to show politeness even when they are voicing disagreement?**
- **How do they signal to interrupt, ask a question or make a point?**

Practice

Practice outside class to improve your discussion skills. Start in an informal setting or with a small group. Begin by asking questions of fellow students. Ask them about the course material. Ask for their opinions. Ask for information or ask for advice.

Participate

If you find it difficult to participate in tutorial discussion, set yourself goals and aim to increase your contribution each week. An easy way to participate is to add to the existing discussion.

Start by making small contributions; agree with what someone has said or ask them to expand on their point (ask for an example or for more information); prepare a question to ask beforehand. You can then work up to answering a question put to the group, providing an example for a point under discussion, or disagreeing with a point.

What is an argument?

To 'argue' in an academic context is to present an opinion through the process of reasoning, supported by evidence.

An argument seeks to persuade through rational and critical judgment. In academic writing an argument is sometimes called a claim or a thesis statement, which is also supported with evidence.

How do we argue at university?

The everyday meaning of the term argument implies a fight: an aggressive conflict or confrontation between adversaries, where one tries to dominate the other in order to 'win'. At university this kind of arguing is not appropriate. The aim of academic argument is to explore a question, proposition or an area of knowledge and achieve reasoned mutual understanding. It is not important who''wins'—what matters most is the quality of the argument itself.

Voicing an Opinion in a Seminar

Participating in a tutorial discussion can be a bit scary, especially when you want to disagree with a point of view and are not sure how to, or of which language structures to use.

Voicing your opinion and using effective arguing techniques are valuable skills.

You may have a great idea, but you need to communicate it effectively and support it. The three essential parts to a point of view are:

1. *A valid opinion (a believable point of view)*

    I believe that ...

    I think that ...

    From what I understand ...

    As I understand it ...

2. *A reason why*

This is due to ...

Because ...

What I mean by this is ...

3. *Evidence (relevant and up-to-date examples, statistics, explanations and/ or expert opinions). If you have actual data, examples or expert opinions on hand, refer to the source.*

This can be seen by

For instance ...

For example ...

An example can be seen ...

(Author's name) states that ...

(Author's name) suggests...

Statistics from (give a source) indicate ...

Arguing a Point : How to disagree effectively

Disagreeing can be problematic as people often speak before they think things through. It is also important to disagree politely. You may be trying to disprove another speaker's point, but

1. *Acknowledge their point*

I can see your point—however ...

That's a good point, but ...

I see what you're getting at, but ...

2. *Then explain why you disagree*

That's not always the case because ...

That's not neccessarily true because ...

This idea isn't supported by statistics/ evidence ...

I thought the author meant that ...

3. *Offer your opinion complete with reason and support*

From what I've read ...

The statistics seem to show that ...

I think what Smith may actually be suggesting is ...

Other studies by Smith show that ...

Now, be prepared for counter-argument and further discussion!

Remember, confidence is the key. If you do your tutorial preparation and think things through, you can speak with confidence and believe that your contribution will be convincing.

Tips for GD

- **Be as natural as possible**. Do not try and be someone you are not. Be yourself so the employer gets to know the real you. A group discussion is your chance to be **more vocal**. The point of interest to the evaluator is to hear you speak.
- Take time to **think of what you are going to say** - if allowed, take a piece of paper and a pen with you and jot down your thoughts, before verbalising them. This could help you create the right framework for your discussion.
- If you have any doubts regarding the subject or about what another team member has said, **ask for clarification**. Don't start speaking until you have **clearly understood and analysed the subject**.
- Work out **various strategies to help you make an entry**: initiate the discussion or agree with someone else's point and then move onto express your views.
- Do not be swayed when you are told that opening the discussion is the only way of gaining attention and recognition. If you do not **give valuable insights during the discussion**, all your efforts of initiating the discussion will be in vain.
- The score you receive depends not only on your verbal communication, but also on **non-verbal skills.** Your body language says a lot about you - your gestures and mannerisms are more likely to reflect your attitude than what you say.
- **Language skills** are important only to the effect as to how you get your points across clearly and fluently.
- **Be assertive** not dominating; try to maintain a balanced tone in your discussion and analysis.
- Be patient; don't lose your cool if anyone says anything you object to. The key is to stay objective: Don't take **the discussion personally.**
- **Always be polite:** Try to avoid using extreme phrases like: 'I strongly object' or 'I disagree'. Instead try phrases like: 'I would like to share my views on…' or 'One difference between your point and mine…'
- Brush up on your **leadership skills**; motivate the other members of the team to speak, and listen to their views. Be receptive to others' opinions and do not be abrasive or aggressive.

- If you have a group of like-minded friends, you can have a mock group discussion where you can learn from each other through giving and receiving feedback.
- Apart from the above points, the panel will also judge team members for their alertness and presence of mind, problem-solving abilities, ability to work as a team without alienating certain members, and creativity. As discussed above.
- **Don't be disheartened if you don't make it after your first group discussion... the best possible preparation for a group discussion is to learn from your past mistakes...**

THE HINDU
Online edition of India's National Newspaper
Wednesday, Jan 17, 2007

Article, Dated January 17, 2007 ,*(Questions answered on career concerns)*. **The FAQ column deals with career concerns addressed to the C&K Management Ltd. P.O. Box 2178, Secunderabad 500003**

I want to know how to prepare for a GD (group discussion) especially when I go for MBA admissions.

Sethuraman
Tambaram

Do not try and be someone you are not – Be as natural as possible. A group discussion is your chance to express your views and be heard. Take time to think of what you are going to say, preferably jotting a few points as this could help you create the right framework for your discussion.

If you have any doubts regarding the subject or about what another team member has said, ask for clarification. In an open discussion it is always possible to gain attention if you give valuable insights. The marks you score depend not only on your verbal communication, but also on your non-verbal skills. Be assertive but not dominating. Try to maintain a balanced tone in your discussion and analysis.

Try to avoid using phrases like: I strongly object' or 'I disagree'. Be receptive to others' opinions and do not be uncompromising.

Apart from these you will also be judged for alertness and presence of mind. Don't be disheartened if you do not do well in your first group discussion. The best possible preparation for a group discussion is to learn from your past mistakes.

How can you contribute to our company? Is there any right way to answer this question?

Vijay Mary
Madurai

To answer this question you require a two-step preparation: assessing your skills and researching the needs of the company. An integral part of skill assessment is looking at your own experience, education and talents to match the job. Consider the job opening, what are the skills needed?

Make a list of the requisite skills (in priority order) and then list concrete examples of your possession of the skill. For 'proof' of this skill, you could list experiences and examples of how you were successful in a difficult situation. These matched skills are your key selling points.

The next step would be based on your research. What are the needs that you can meet? In other words, given the specifics of the company, what value can you add? After these two steps, you will be in a better position to come up with concrete examples of what you can offer the company.

Opening Our Eyes To Differences Among Group Members

Extroverts and introverts: A Question of Style

Persons who embrace an **extroverted** communication style like to think out loud, composing their thoughts on the fly. They may be uncomfortable with silence in a group.

Persons who embrace an **introverted** communication style like to think privately on an issue, listen to what everyone else has to say, and then speak their mind. They often are comfortable with extended periods of silence in a group.

A balance of group contributions occurs when group members appreciate varied communication styles while encouraging each other to step out of form on occasion: persons who favor an extroverted style need to periodically relax and silently ruminate about an issue; persons who favor an introverted style need periodically to be encouraged to contribute, even if they haven't worked out the problem fully in their heads yet.

Gender and cultural differences

Groups work together best when group members experiment with a variety of roles in groups, even those with which they don't have as much experience.

Sometimes differences in cultural backgrounds make group communication difficult. Typical cultural differences in patterns of communication include greater or less degrees of bluntness, greater or less assertiveness in speech, and a preference for either direct conversation or for roundabout and indirect conversation.

Groups work together best when members exercise a sensitivity to these differences, value their uniqueness, and remain open to talking to each other despite their differences.

Minefields of Ego-think and Clone-think:

Group work can become frustrating if a group member puts all his or her energy into expressing his or her view and no energy at all into listening to others and reaching understanding as a group.

But group work misfires also when a group member puts no energy at all into the group effort, quickly agreeing with the first statement offered and deciding that the conversation is over.

Effective groups monitor the energy levels in their conversation: there is a middle road between the monopolizing tendencies of **Egothink** and the passive stances of **Clonethink**.

What leads to an excellent discussion?

All members agree to an extended conversation in which all share their views. When they move gradually but steadily toward the integration and synthesis of views, creative, high-energy, and effective learning occurs among all members of the group.

Role Play

Role play is a teaching strategy that allows one to practice a variety of communication skills by performing real life situation. Each role play has characters through which a story is developed. It can be situational which acts as simulation sharpening your decision making skills.

Role playing is a useful technique for thinking about difficult situations before they occur, so that you have good pre-prepared responses for the different eventualities that can arise. Role-playing can also be used to analyze problems from different perspectives, to spark brainstorming sessions, to experiment with different solutions to a problem, to develop team work, and help group problem-solving. Role-playing happens when a group of people act out roles in a particular scenario. The scenario is usually based on a problem that needs a solution, a situation that needs to be more closely examined, or a case or issue that demands a different perspective.

Although role-playing is common in communication training, there are no reports about the use of student role-plays in the training of technical skills. Role-playing is widely used as a method in the field of communication training (e.g Cauhan & Long, 2000; Magnani et al., 2002; Nikendei et al., 2003) and focuses on the interaction between participants (Tolan & Lendrum, 1995). There are at least two simulative components of role-playing: the "deputy acting" (Kochan, 1981) and the "as-if actions and circumstances" (Yardley-Matwiejczuk, 1997). With these methods participants take on a particular role in a simulated true-life context, acting as-if they were another person in a given situation. Here risk-free practice becomes possible (Simpson, 1985). Furthermore, the practice of immediate feedback following role-playing is of high didactic value (Tolan & Lendrum, 1995).

Elocution

It is oratorical or expressive delivery of speech, including intonation, gestures and style of speaking or delivery. Lets practice !

Want to improve your voice? /Ever thought you'd like to sound clearer when you speak?/ Like to get more variety into your voice?

Ever thought of how you might have sounded if you took elocution lessons as a child?

Elocution Lesson One - Breathing & Relaxation
Firstly we are going to try and relax and take a few deep breaths. OK? And when you breathe in deeply try not to move your shoulders too much but breathe in from your belly (or stomach).

Ready? OK ...Breathe in ..... deeply ... remember to use your stomach ... and now wait a few seconds .... then breathe out slowly .... and count out aloud as you do it ...

... 1 ... 2 ... 3 ... 4 ... 5 ... 6... 7 ... 8 ... 9 ... 10 ... ... 11 ... 12 ... 13 ... 14 ... 15 ... 16 ... 17 ... 18 ... 19 ... 20. Try and count all the way to 20 as you breathe out. OK normal breath in again ... and out.

Now lets try the deep breathing exercise again and count slowly all the way to 20.

So ... Breathe in ..... deeply ... and ... wait a few seconds .... then breathe out slowly .... and count out aloud as you do it ... 1 ... 2 ... 3 ... 4 ... 5 ... 6... 7 ... 8 ... 9 ... 10 ...... 11 ... 12 ... 13 ... 14 ... 15 ... 16 ... 17 ... 18 ... 19 ... 20..... try and count all the way to 20 as you breathe out.

Elocution Lesson Two - Text Reading

How about reading out some text aloud? OK? Find yourself a room where you wont be disturbed - or overheard! Now read the following paragraph:

It was a beautiful day in more ways than one when Harry finally decided to ask c to marry him. The Summer weather had now settled down and although there were still a few clouds in the sky, it was a very bright, blue sky that greeted them as they left the motel. Gerry took Sally by the arm and embrased her. And in that moment, he knew they were meant for each other.

Now read it again but this time t7hink about how much your mouth is opening. Try and open your mouth as wide as possible when you speak each word. In fact try and speak each word individually and not as part of a sentence. Try and make each word sound clear as possible. Try and "spit" out each of the words.

What we are trying to do there is to make each word have a beginning and an end. Oftentimes when we speak we "slurrrrrr" our speech and do not take enough effort to pronounce each word clearly enough.

So lets repeat the paragraph one more time. This time reading it as a whole piece of text (not individual words without meaning) and making it sound as exciting (and emotional) a moment for Jerry as you possibly can. **And how did that sound to you?**

Elocution Lesson Three - Tongue Twisters

"Three grey geese in a green field grazing"

And again ... read it out aloud and faster. Dont worry if you get mixed up with some of the words just try it again a few times till you can say it out loud ten times in 30 seconds. And remember to open your mouth as much as possible.

Now lets try another phrase. And of course you know the routine now ... so try this one:-

"a proper copper coffee pot"

Read it out aloud 10 times yet?

Are you starting to feel as if your jaw, mouth and tongue are getting some exercise?

If not then you need to try the two tongue twisters again!

Elocution Lesson Four - Recap

Now lets go back to the start.

What you have been doing (in a simplistic way) by the above exercise is a warm up. Many presenters, actors and public speakers spend lots of time in vocal exercises like that before going on stage or reading the news or giving a presentation so that when they start speaking to the audience they have already warmed up their voice and are able to "hit the road running".

A lot of what you do in elocution lessons is similar to this. You'll also work on specific vowel sounds (a, e, i, o, u) and constanants (b, c, d, f, g, h, ... etc). These exercises will help you change the way some of your words sounds to the ear (vowel sounds) and also help you pronounce words more clearly (constanant sounds). You can use these exercises to soften or even (over time) lose an accent.

Next Steps ... Elocution Coach?

Remember developing a great voice takes time and dedication. But there's nothing to stop you starting to improve your own voice right now. In fact ... you have done just that if you actually took part in these exercises above.

... and if you didnt actually try out the exercises ...

... but just skimmed through them silently ... Why not try them?

... what have you got to lose?

We rarely read aloud these days. Why not start doing this. Pick up a paper or magazine and read some of the text out aloud. Not in front of people - otherwise they might think you a bit strange! But in the comfort of your own home. **Spend about 5 - 10 minutes a day reading out aloud** ... and by the end of your first week will not only have got used to doinig this you will start to enjoy hearing the sound of your voice. You will also be on the road to achieving more from your voice.

And when you are reading the text in the papers or magazines ... try and experiment reading them out with different emotions. Be angry ... be mysterious ... be humorous ... and note how the tone of your voice changes when you change your emotions. And if you have the chance try recording yourself again.

Imprompto : While many of us do not like to speak in front of people, there are times when we are asked to get up and say a few words about someone or a topic when we have not planned on saying anything at all. We are more shocked than anyone else.

Instantaneous response to a given topic – Here one has have a clear and creative mind to canalize ideas, plan, design, and check your facts as well as acquiring information.

- **Decide quickly what your one message will be** - Keep in mind you have not been asked to give a speech but to make some impromptu remarks. Hopefully they have asked you early enough so you can at least jot down a few notes before you speak. If not, pick ONE message or comment and focus on that one main idea. Many times, other ideas may come to you after you start speaking. If this happens, go with the flow and trust your instincts.
- **Do not try and memorize what you will say** - Trying to memorize will only make you more nervous and you will find yourself thinking more about the words and not about the message.
- **Start off strong and with confidence** - If you at least plan your opening statement, this will get you started on the right foot. After all, just like with any formal speech, getting started is the most difficult. Plan what your first sentence will be. You may even write this opening line down on your note card and glance at it one more time just before you begin speaking. If you know you have three points or ideas to say, just start off simple by saying, "I would just like to talk about 3 points". The first point is... the second point is... and so on.
- **Decide on your transitions from one point to the other** - After you have decided on your opening remark or line, come up with a simple transition statement that takes you to your main point. If you have more than one point to make, you can use a natural transition such as, "My second point is... or my next point is..." etc. Just list on your note card or napkin, if you have to, the main points or ideas. Do not write out the exact words, but just the points you want to mention.
- **Maintain eye contact with the audience** - This is easier to do if you do not write down all kinds of stuff to read. Look down at your next idea or thought and maintain eye contact with your audience and speak from your heart. Focus on communicating TO your audience and not speaking AT the crowd.

- **Occasionally Throw in an off-the-cuff remark** - Because you want your style to be flexible and seem impromptu, trust your instinct and add a few words which just pop into your head. Keep it conversational and think of the audience as a group of your friends.
- **Finally, have a good conclusion** - Gracefully just state, "And the last point I would like to make is ....". Once you have made your last point, you can then turn control back to the person who asked you to speak in the first place.

CHAPTER - 4

INTERPERSONAL SKILLS

Interpersonal skills

In today's team-based organizations, winning the respect and cooperation of bosses, colleagues or staff members is critical if you want people to help you get things done. That's why interpersonal skills are essential to your own effectiveness as a manager.

In this book, you'll discover how perceptions influence your interactions with others and their responses to you...identify and flex your interpersonal style...use listening and feedback skills to build understanding...assertively manage conflict and turn potential adversaries into allies...direct and motivate others to high levels of performance...develop give-and-take relationships that produce results!

Interpersonal skill comprises of:

A. Leadership

The process of successfully influencing the activities of a group towards the achievement of a common goal. A leader has the ability to influence others through qualities such as personal charisma, expertise, command of language, and the creation of mutual respect. As well as requiring strong Communication Skills and Personal Skills, leadership uses the Background skills of the following.

(a) *Mentoring is :* Being a trusted advisor and helper with experience in a particular field. Actively supporting and guiding someone to develop knowledge and experience, or to achieve career or personal goals (for example, a third-year student mentoring a first year student, helping to adjust to the university experience).

A mentoring relationship may be formal or informal, but must involve trust, mutual respect, and commitment as both parties work together to achieve a goal (for example, mentoring a younger member of a team to achieve better performance in the lead-up to a sporting event).

B. **Team Work**
- **(a)** *Group work is :* Any activity in which students work together; any activity which has been specifically designed so that students work in pairs or groups, and may be assessed as a group (referred to as formal group work); or when students come together naturally to help each other with their work (referred to as informal group work). Peer group activity in lab classes, tutorials etc
- **(b)** *Decision making is :* Identifying appropriate evidence and weighing up that evidence to make a choice (for example, gathering and assessing information to find the best way to perform an experiment).

  Taking responsibility for a decision and its outcomes (for example, choosing a topic for a group presentation from a number of suggestions).
- **(c)** *Delegation is :* Taking responsibility for determining when to ask someone else to make a decision or carry out a task (for example, figuring out what is a fair distribution of the workload in a group project, and sharing responsibility with others).

  Distributing responsibility and authority in a group by giving someone else the discretion to make decisions that you have the authority to make (for example, as the chosen leader of a lab experiment team, you could assign tasks and decisions to different group members).
- **(d)** *Collaboration is :* Working cooperatively and productively with other team members to contribute to the outcomes of the team's work (for example, dividing the workload and sharing the results of your own work with others in the group, or assisting members of the group who are having difficulty completing their tasks).

C. **Networking**
- **(a)** **Network building** is: Creating contacts with other people and maintaining those contacts (for example, meeting someone at a seminar with similar interests, and swapping email addresses with them).

  Acquiring and maintaining information about people who might be useful contacts for specific purposes (for example, seeking out people established in an industry you hope to work with one day).

Using a contact in an ethical manner to help each of you meet specific goals, (for example, collaborating on projects of importance to both of you).

(b) *Motivating others is :* Generating enthusiasm and energy by being positive, focusing on finding solutions and maintaining a positive attitude even when things are not going well (for example, when something goes wrong, asking "What can we try now?" instead of saying, "That should have worked better.").

Encouraging others to come up with solutions, listening carefully to their ideas and offering constructive feedback (for example, gathering suggestions for a group project, and giving each person's ideas fair discussion).

Being prepared to support others in taking agreed, calculated risks, and not blaming others when things go wrong (for example, one group member's portion of a presentation receives a poor mark - make sure that this student isn't blamed by the group, and focus on learning from the mistakes).

D. **Body Language**
- Nonverbal communication, known as "body language" sends strong positive and negative signals. This is how much it influences any message:

Words	8%
Tone of voice	34%
Non-verbal cues	58%
Message	100%

Body language includes…

- Face
- Focus
- Tone
- Figure
- Territory
- Time

Face includes:
- Your expressions
- Your smile or lack thereof
- Tilt of the head; e.g., if your head is tilted to one side, it usually indicates you are interested in what someone is saying

What message are you sending if someone is presenting a new idea and you are frowning?

Figure includes:
- Your posture
- Your demeanor and gestures
- Your clothes and accessories such as jewelry

What message are you sending if you are dressed casually at an important meeting?

Focus *is your eye contact with others*
- *The perception of eye contact differs by culture. For most Americans...*
  - Staring makes other people uncomfortable
  - Lack of eye contact can make you appear weak or not trustworthy
  - Glasses may interfere or enhance eye contact

What message are you sending if you are looking at other things and people in a room when someone is speaking to you?

Territory focuses on how you use space. It is also called proxemics.
- The perception of territory differs by culture. Most Americans are comfortable with an individual space that is about an arm's length in diameter

What message are you sending if you keep moving closer to a person who is backing away from you?

Tone is a factor of your voice
- Pitch is the highness or lowness of voice
- Volume is how loud your voice is
- Emphasis is your inflection

What message are you sending if during a disagreement you start speaking very loudly?

Time focuses on how you use time. It is also called chronemics.
- Pace is how quickly you speak
- Response is how quickly you move
- Punctuality is your timeliness

What message are you sending if you are consistently late for meetings?

You may have heard that actions speak louder than words. What does that mean? It means that what you do often means more than what you say. What you do is nonverbal language. It can be gestures. It can be what you wear. It can be other things. It is another way to communicate. People shows feelings and attitudes through nonverbal cues. People say that they believe nonverbal cues more than spoken words.

The context of a nonverbal cue helps you get the right meaning. Individual and cultural differences affect how nonverbal cues are sent and received. There are many types of nonverbal cues. Most are habits. You may not be know what messages you send. You may not understand the messages others send you

> **It has been estimated that 97% of all college students have never studied** the art of nonverbal communication. They will go through life, just like everyone else, missing out on what is actually being said. Over 97% of the population is unaware of the communications skills you will learn in our workshops. Imagine the advantages your staff would have if they knew these skills.

Body posture and walk. Standing straight shows confidence. Slouching shows disregard. It looks like you don't care. Crossing your arms over your chest shows you have a closed mind. It can also mean that you are protecting yourself or are disobedient. Arms at your side show openness. Walking is body posture in motion. How you walk—speed and movement—tells something about you. Your body posture and walk should be different at home than at work. At work, You should look like you are ready and eager to work. Watch others on the job to see how they look.

If you're a manager, it's imperative that you be aware of your body signals and tone to ensure that they correspond with your message. For example, if you shift your eyes and look away while speaking, people won't trust your message. If you raise your voice in a questioning tone while giving out quotas, you'll sound as though you don't believe they're achievable.

I once worked with a manager whose department had a terrible morale problem. He had asked his staff what they wanted from him. They requested that he drop by their offices once in a while and also schedule regular meetings with them. The manager did both, but the morale got worse.

When I came in to study the situation, I found that the man's body language was causing all of the problems. It was domineering. When he dropped into people's offices, he'd take up the whole doorway or walk up to their desks and look them in the eye—even if they were on the phone! People found his behavior unnerving. It sent the message that their personal space belonged to him. At meetings, the manager would place his hands behind his head, cross his legs, lean back, and look at the ceiling. That body language said that he already had all of the answers.

After I pointed out what messages his body language was sending, the manager changed his behavior and boosted everyone's morale.

Facial Expression. Facial expression is the visual form of tone. Your face shows your mood. It shows boredom. It shows anger. It shows sadness. It shows what you feel. Like tone, you can learn to have professional facial expressions.

Eye contact. Looking people in the eye shows that you trust them and they can trust you. It shows your interest. When you don't look at people, they think you don't care.

Tone. Tone of voice shows attitude. A voice can sound bored, excited, angry, mean, and so on. It shows feelings.

You need different tones for different contexts. You use a different tone at home than at work. At work, you need a professional tone. What does that sound like? By varying the tone of certain words, we change the meaning of our statements and questions.

For example, take the statement, "I didn't tell her to come to the party." Saying, "I didn't tell her to come to the party" suggests that someone else told her to come. Saying, "I didn't tell *her* to come to the party" insinuates that you may have suggested she come, but you didn't tell her to. Saying, "I didn't tell her to come to the *party*" implies that you told someone else to come to the party. "I didn't tell her to *come* to the party" indicates that you told her to come to another event. As you can see, the tone of certain words results in different interpretations.

Tone of voice is especially important in customer service. If you interact with customers frequently, you need to be aware of the message you're conveying. Do you do everything possible to help customers, or does your voice tell them to move on so you can help the next person? A client of mine has a plaque in his office that states, "The phone is not an interruption of your work. It is the reason you are here."

Distance. A kind of invisible line surrounds each person. When people cross the line, that person feels uncomfortable.

They get too close for comfort. Distance is affected by context. You get closer to someone you love than to a stranger. You get closer to a co-worker than to a boss.

Hand gestures. Gestures are symbols.

They have meanings. A handshake means that a bargain is sealed. A raised fist shows anger. Thumbs-up shows readiness.

Body gestures. Shrugging your shoulders shows that you don't know or don't care. Tapping a foot shows your impatience. Hands on your hips shows anger. Nodding your head shows agreement.

From 65 to 90 percent of every conversation is interpreted through body language, says Ray Birdswhistell, professor of research in anthropology at Temple University and author of numerous books on body language. We react more to what we think someone meant than to the words he or she said.

If someone tells you, "You're doing a great job!" with a smile on her face and a relaxed body, you'll probably believe her. On the other hand, if that person says, "You're doing a great job!" with gritted teeth, a half smile, and a stiff body, you may be unsure about the true message. Most likely, you'll feel that you aren't working up to par, but you won't be sure why.

Types of Nonverbal Communication

7 Cs of body language

- **Cluster** – Gestures come in clusters. Do not view in isolation
- **Context** – Different situations would entail different interpretations
- **Congruence** – Look for at least three of the seven components to see if the signals are congruent
- **Control** – Look for controlled or fake gestures
- **Culture** - Be sensitive to cultural difference
- **Commonality** – Most gestures are universal
- **Caution** – Many expressions are fleeting. You would have to increase your awareness level to catch them

Exercise : OBSERVING NONVERBAL COMMUNICATION

Watch yourself in different situations. Get others (inmate, teacher, supervisor) to watch you when you are unaware. See how you communicate nonverbally. Determine if how you look is what you mean.

OBSERVER : Self _____ Other (name) _____

SITUATION : Work (type) _____ Class Meal_____

Home/Other _____

Describe each of the following and tell what they meant:

BODY POSTURE AND WALK

VOCAL TONE

DISTANCE

HAND GESTURES

BODY GESTURES

FACIAL EXPRESSION

EYE CONTACT

APPEARANCE

Chapter - 5

RESUME WRITING

Preparing a resume is one of those tasks that sounds easy but actually takes time and skill. One false move here, and you could blow your chances for that perfect career.

A little extra effort, you can create a resume that makes you really stand out as a superior candidate for a job you are seeking. Not one resume in a hundred follows the principles that stir the interest of prospective employers. So, even if you face fierce competition, with a well written resume you should be invited to interview more often than many people more qualified than you.

To understand what I mean, let's take a look at the purpose of your resume. Why do you have a resume in the first place? What is it supposed to do for you?

The resume is a tool with one specific purpose: to win an interview. If it does what the fantasy resume did, it works. If it doesn't, it isn't an effective resume. A resume is an advertisement, nothing more, nothing less.

A great resume doesn't just tell them what you have done but makes the same assertion that all good ads do: If you buy this product, you will get these specific, direct benefits. It presents you in the best light. Your resume is a matchmaker. Once you are convinced that there is a mutual match between job expectations and your profile, your resume should aim at **projecting you in an appropriate manner.** It convinces the employer that you have what it takes to be successful in this new position or career.

Potential employers receive hundreds of applications and resumes every time they post a new position within their organization. With this in mind, one must choose a resume that is going to promote him or her in the most favorable light. It is advised that a person take some time to think and plan out what skills and experience they have to offer before drafting his or her resume. Knowing where to place education verse experience; using an objective or a summary; listing dates or omitting them; are all very important questions one must answer if they desire to be competitive for employment. Often it is the first impression you will make on a prospective employer. Hopefully, after looking over your resume, the employer will grant you the opportunity to make a second impression.

What is a Resume

A Resume is a self-promotional document that presents you in the best possible light, for the purpose of getting invited to a job interview.

It's not an official personnel document. It's not a job application. It's not a "career obituary"! And it's not a confessional.

What is a well written resume?

- Comprehensive and conveys all the important details at a glance.
- Grabs the interest of the employer.
- Enables the prospective employer to form a good first impression.
- Sets the tone of discussion during the interview.
- Is SIMPLE, ACCURATE, COMPLETE in information

Types of Resume

The most common resume styles are:

- **Chronological Format**

    The Chronological Resume is perhaps the most widely used resume style, especially by college graduates. The standard Chronological Resume is comprised of four main sections: the Heading, Objective, Education, and Experience

    Easy to read, most commonly used

    Presents education and work experience in reverse chronological order

    The reason behind this format is based on the idea that new graduates rely heavily on their Academic work as their only experience. By listing courses that pertain to the position applied for, one can demonstrate that he or she has the knowledge to carry out such a position if hired. Older persons may decide to down play his or her education for a variety of reasons, and therefore education would be placed behind experience in the final layout.

Experts in the resume writing industry now suggest omitting information about one's hobbies or special interests unless they are directly related to the position applied for. Placing names of referees is also something that was done in the past, which experts now suggest also leaving out. Findings suggest that these components can hinder one's chances of obtaining an interview, thus disqualifying them before he or she has a chance to meet face to face with the employer.

- *Functional Format*

    A functional resume categorizes skills by function, emphasizing your abilities. This is useful if you are changing careers and want to show how you can transfer your skills. As stated previously, it is important to show prospective employers what you can offer them. A functional resume does just that. A functional job objective is given first, followed by several paragraphs, each discussing a different job function

    Focuses on skills and abilities, not dates of employment. Lists skills you've demonstrated which are required for a particular job. Allows you to emphasize skills gained through volunteer work and extra curricular activities

    The Functional Resume is helpful for those who have large employment gaps or several extensive major accomplishments. The Functional Resume also plays down educational achievements, which is why it is often listed at the end. If the purpose of a resume were to obtain an interview, it would be recommended to stay away from this format if possible.

- *Combination Format*

    A combination resume is exactly what it sounds like — it combines a functional resume with a chronological one. An objective is listed at the top, after your name and address, of course. Following that are paragraphs describing job functions. A section titled "Employment Experience" comes next. That is where the chronological part of the resume comes in. List employers and dates in this section. Do not offer further descriptions here as you have already described your abilities in the functional part of this resume. This is a useful format if you are changing careers but have a solid employment history. I also find it useful if your job duties on a single job were very diverse and you want to stress your various abilities. If you spent a long time at one job but moved up through the company, you might want to use a combination resume

Uses elements of Chronological and Functional

Emphasizes skills and abilities

Provides job/experience descriptions

- ***Technical Format***

   Used as a term to describe a resume prepared for technical positions (e.g. computer science or engineering). The technical resume is only used in cases where mentioning particular skills or knowledge of a technical nature is particularly important, as is the case for the IT Industry. The technical resume should be very much like the chronological resume, except it must include a summary of skill, preferably at the beginning of the resume.

   This type of resume is the only one that should use jargon and technological terms. If the position you are applying for requires experience in using certain equipment or having particular skills, then this is where you mention it and if possible quantify it. Generally, if a position requires a specific skill, employers will mention it on their job description or advertisement.

   If you have experience in a technical area that you think is important for the position, or will give you an advantage over other applicants, then make sure you mention it. It is also very important to list your qualifications and to include any courses, training or seminars you have attended, particularly where they are requirements for the position.

   Just remember that jargon and technical language should be avoided throughout the resume. The only safe place to mention it is on the summary of skills page. Often the first person that reads the resume is not a technical person, but a Recruitment Officer, you don't want to write yourself off by submitting a resume that they cannot understand, however the summary of skills allows you to use more specific technological language.

When preparing the summary of skills page, try and group items together with sub-headings so that it is easier to follow. That would make it easier for the reader to find the specific details he is looking for. Be brief and use point form whenever possible.

Can use any format; emphasizes technical skills such as specific computer languages, laboratory skills.

- **Curriculum Vitae**

   A curriculum vitae – often called a CV or vita – tends to be used more for scientific and teaching positions than a resume. Thus, vitas tend to provide great detail about academic and research experiences. Where resumes tend toward brevity, vitas lean toward completeness. Unlike resumes, there is no set format to vitas

   Used by individuals seeking teaching and/or research positions in a post-secondary institution or high-level research industry. Often two or three pages for master's or doctoral degree candidates.

   The Chronological format is widely preferred by employers, and works well if you're staying in the same field . Only use a Functional format if you're changing fields, and you're sure a skills-oriented format would show off your transferable skills to better advantage; and **be sure** to include a clear chronological work history.

A good objective statement answers questions
- What position(s) are you applying for?
- What are your main qualifications?
- What are your career goals?
- What is your professional identity?

How can a student list summer jobs?

Students can make their resume look neater by listing seasonal jobs very simply, such as "Spring 1996" or "Summer 1996" rather than 6/96 to 9/96. (The word "Spring" can be in very tiny letters, say 8-point in size.)

What if you don't quite have your degree or credentials yet?

You can say something like: Eligible for U.S. credentials — **or**

Graduate studies in Instructional Design, in progress — **or**

Master's Degree anticipated December 1997.

Resume Writing

A few things to remember...

There is really **no ONE right way** to write a resume—everyone is unique. There is room to "be yourself."

Proofread your resume very carefully for grammar, punctuation, and spelling. You do not want ANY mistakes in your resume. Have someone review your resume for mistakes and use spell check!

Get **feedback** from other people. Make sure that your resume looks good, is easy to understand, and says what you want it to say!

How To Write  Resume

1. Begin resume by writing your full name, address, telephone number, fax and email at the top of the resume.
2. Write an objective. The objective is a short sentence describing what type of work you hope to obtain.
3. Begin work experience with your most recent job. Include the company specifics and your responsibilities - **focus on the skills.**
4. Continue to list all of your work experience job by job progressing backwards in time. Remember to focus on skills that are transferable.
5. Summarize your education, including important facts (degree type, specific courses studied) that are applicable to the job you are applying for.

6. Include other relevant information such as languages spoken, computer programming knowledge, Hobbies etc. under the heading: **Extra Curricular Skills**
7. Finish with the phrase: REFERENCES Available upon request
8. Your entire resume should ideally not be any longer than one page. If you have had a number of years of experience specific to the job you are applying for, two pages are also acceptable.

Elements of a Resume

- *Objective*

    A targeted statement that clearly states the type of job you are seeking. Gives resume focus, credibility and direction

    Good objectives are very specific—

    "To work with the design and development of new computer systems with a special interest in microprocessor application." "Position in public opinion polling or consumer product market research using skills in survey design and statistical analysis."

    OR

    "To utilize my academic training in order to attain a responsible and challenging position as an Software engineer,where as I can contribute for the overall growth of the organization and myself by utilizing my abilities"

    Objectives are optional.

    Avoid cliches such as "like working with people"

Focus on You	Focus on the Position
Skills	Industry
Education	Job Title(s)
Goals	Type of Organization
	Geographic Area

- **Summary of Qualifications/Skills (Profile)**

    A summary of relevant skills, knowledge and accomplishments. Be specific! Tailor this section to the job to which you're applying. If it is well written, this section can really help a potential employer to focus on your strengths. Think carefully about what you have to offer.

- **Education**

  Include degrees, expected date of completion if you have not finished, relevant coursework, and honors and awards (placed under the appropriate degree)

  List highest degree first, followed by other degrees received

  Degree level

  Major(s), minor(s) and emphasis if applicable

  If your major/degree is relevant, list that first; if not, emphasize then list major. You might also consider placing your "Experience" section first.

- **Experience**

  Think in terms of experience, not employment or work history.

  Be sure to include internships and unpaid positions if they are relevant.

  Be concise in your descriptions of what you did.

  Do not use "Responsibilities included" or "Duties were."

  Translate specialized skills and interests into everyday language

- **Some additional/optional categories:**
  - Professional memberships/Leadership/Community Activities/Leadership
  - (Computer) skills
  - Publications/Presentations (much briefer than on a CV)
  - Additional Information
  - Honors/Awards/Hobbies/Interests- Avoid listing those which may be controversial

- **References**
  - Usually state "References Provided Upon Request" as last line of resume
  - Provide separate sheet with three - four reference names and contact information
  - No relatives, friends, other students
  - Ask permission before listing someone

Personal Data
- Date of Birth/Age
- Medical History
- Height/Weight
- Marital Status
- Race/Ethnicity
- Willingness to Reloca

General Guidelines

Length
- Generally one page (especially recent grads)
- Two pages with extensive related experience

Layout
- Direct reader's eye using headings and layout
- Choose standard font in 10-14 point size
- Use appropriate color & high quality 8 1/2 x 11 paper, one-sided only!
- Leave 'white space' for uncluttered look
- One inch margins on all sides is standard
- Be consistent with:
  - indentations
  - capitalizations
  - font
  - spacing

Content–Proofread! Don't rely on Spell-check
- grammar
- spelling
- typographical errors
- punctuation

Stress accomplishments and results

Tailor contents to each position (e.g. rewrite Objective/revise Skills section)

Omit information which could be used in a discriminatory way (e.g., religious affiliations, age, etc.)

Identifying Information

- Put your name, permanent and campus addresses, permanent and campus phone numbers, and email address prominently at the top of your resume.
- Avoid using a nickname to identify yourself.
- Consider including your URL address or fax number if you have one

Words of Advice

We've entered an era when very talented and competent people are not getting jobs. The only remedy is to stand out and self-promote. If you do, you'll always get the nod over those who do not."

Jeffrey Davidson, Marketing Consultant

Resume Dos

- DO think of your resume as an ad for your qualifications, not an autobiography.
- DO begin each bullet point with a verb.
- DO included paid and unpaid experience to demonstrate the range of what you've done.
- DO show the reader why you're a good match for a particular job.
- DO make several resumes, with each one targeting a particular field.
- DO look at other resumes to see how they are written
- DO use reverse chronology (the most recent position is your first entry) to organize your education and experience.
- DO format your resume clearly.
- DO proofread many times.
- DO ask others to look at your resume.
- DO come to Career Services for a critique.
- DO remember that most employers will only look at your resume for 15-30 seconds.

Resume Don'ts

- DON'T make your reader dig for information.
- DON'T tell everything you've ever done.
- DON'T use complete sentences
- DON'T include personal information, such as age, race, marital or health status.
- DON'T make your resume too dense, busy or cute.
- DON'T use a font smaller than 10 point.
- DON'T use fancy fonts that are hard to read.

Resume Format For A Fresher

RESUME

                     Address   :

                     Ph   :

                     Mobile   :

                     E-Mail   :

Name Of the Candidate
CAREER OBJECTIVE:

ACADEMIC QUALIFICATION

S.No	COURSE	INSTITUTION/BOARD	YEAR OF PASSING	PERCENTAGE

COMPUTER SKILLS :

TRAITS:

ACHIEVEMENTS:

PROJECTS :

EXTRA CURRICULAR ACTIVITIES:

PERSONAL DETAILS

Father's Name	:
Date of Birth	:
Sex	:
Languages known	:
Hobbies	:
Passport No.	:

DECLARATION

I hereby declare that the above mentioned information is correct upto my knowledge and I bear the responsibility for the correctness of the above mentioned particulars.

Place:

Date :   **Signature Of the Candidate**

RESUME

12,Govindaswamy Street
George Town
Chennai
Tel No: 044-6123582
e-mail Jyoti_12@yahoo.co.in

Jyoti Ansari

CAREER OBJECTIVE: To work with the design and development of new computer systems with a special interest in microprocessor application." "Position in consumer product market research using skills in survey design and statistical analysis"

ACADEMIC QUALIFICATION

S.No	COURSE	INSTITUTION/BOARD	YEAR OF PASSING	PERCENTAGE
1.	B.E (CSE)	National College Of Engineering, Trichy	1996-2000	78%
2.	Higher Secondary	St.John Sr.Sec School, Trichy	1994-1996	92%
3.	Xth (CBSE Board)	St. John Sr.Sec School, Trichy	1993-1994	98%

COMPUTER SKILLS :   C, C++, Turbo, Jave, .Net.

PROJECTS : Bio-medical Instrumentation and signal processing-a comparative study of cardiac and respiratory rates of human beings and animals leading to the perfecting techniques in treating acute respiratory tract problems in asthma patients

ACHIEVEMENTS: Received Bronze Medal –IIIrd Rank In District –Higher Sec School 1996

EXTRA CURRICULAR ACTIVITIES:

Publication   :   Digital Image Processing- a new approach a paper read at REC, Calicut (Sept 1997)

Seminars   :   Attended a Three Day All India seminar on Techniques in Programming   (Sept 1998)

Sports	:	Represented College in Inter-Badminton Championship in 1997,1998
Cultural / Camps	:	Conducted Blood Donation Camp in College
		Participated In skit for the Annual Day Celebration

PERSONAL DETAILS

Father's Name	:	Mr. K.l Ansari
Date of Birth	:	Feb 7, 1975
Sex	:	Female
Languages known	:	English/ Tamil/ Hindi/ German
Hobbies	:	Reading Books/ Daily Newspaper
Passport No.	:	

DECLARATION

I hereby declare that the above mentioned information is correct upto my knowledge and I bear the responsibility for the correctness of the above mentioned particulars.

Place: **Jyoti**

Date :   Signature of the Candidate

ADD POWER TO YOUR RESUME WITH POWERWORDS

Ability capable capability capacity competence competent complete completely consistent contributions demonstrated developing educated efficient effective effectiveness enlarging equipped excellent exceptional expanding experienced global increasing knowledgeable major mature maturity nationwide outstanding performance positive potential productive proficient profitable proven qualified record repeatedly resourceful responsible results significant significantly sound specialist substantial substantially successful stable thorough thoroughly versatile vigorous well educated well rounded worldwide accelerated accomplished achieved addressed administered advised allocated answered appeared applied appointed appraised approved arranged assessed assigned assisted assumed assured audited awarded

bought briefed broadened brought budgeted built

cataloged caused changed chaired clarified classified closed collected combined commented communicated compared compiled completed computed conceived concluded conducted conceptualized considered consolidated constructed consulted continued contracted controlled converted coordinated corrected counseled counted created critiqued cut

dealt decided defined delegated delivered demonstrated described designed determined developed devised diagnosed directed discussed distributed documented doubled drafted

earned edited effected eliminated endorsed enlarged enlisted ensured entered established estimated evaluated examined executed expanded expedited experienced experimented explained explored expressed extended

filed filled financed focused forecast formulated found founded gathered generated graded granted guided halved handled helped identified implemented improved incorporated increased indexed initiated influenced innovated inspected installed instituted instructed insured interpreted interviewed introduced invented invested investigated involved issued

joined kept

launched learned leased lectured led licensed listed logged made maintained managed matched measured mediated met modified monitored motivated moved named navigated negotiated observed opened operated ordered organized oversaw

participated perceived performed persuaded planned prepared presented processed procured programmed prohibited projected promoted proposed provided published purchased pursued

qualified questioned raised ranked rated realized received recommended reconciled recorded recruited redesigned reduced regulated rehabilitated related reorganized repaired replaced replied reported represented researched resolved responded restored revamped reviewed revise saved scheduled selected served serviced set set up shaped shared showed simplified sold solved sorted sought sparked specified spoke staffed started streamlined strengthened stressed stretched structured studied submitted substituted succeeded suggested summarized superseded supervised surveyed systematized tackled targeted taught terminated tested took toured traced tracked traded trained transferred transcribed transformed translated transported traveled treated trimmed tripled turned tutored umpired uncovered understood understudied unified unraveled updated upgraded used utilized

verbalized verified visited waged weighed widened won worked wrote

The key to writing a good, solid resume is to remember that your resume tells your professional story. It is only one component of obtaining an interview, but it can be the most critical component if you have not done any networking in advance of submitting your resume to a prospective employer. Keep it short, simple, but focused and direct.

A well-written resume is an essential component in helping you stand out against your competition, and will keep your name in the mind of the company you are targeting in your career journey.

Job hunting tips: Choosing a career

Self-knowledge
Making career decisions can be challenging and sometimes graduates struggle to know where to begin. Looking at vacancies is a common starting point but not one that would be advised. Many vacancies are never advertised, so looking at job adverts will only ever give you a biased and partial picture of the graduate labour market.

If you are unsure which career will suit you, you would be better to spend some time thinking about yourself. Become better acquainted with yourself; be aware of your skills, interests and what motivates you. Consider any background issues or constraints, such as mobility, affecting your choice.

You can then start to use this information to identify matching jobs, courses and potential employers. Think about the skills you wish to use at work, your feelings about further study, which working environments appeal to you, the sort of lifestyle you want and so on. Try to tackle this in a structured way:

Talk to a careers adviser in your university careers service.

Make full use of the information on this website, particularly what jobs would suit me? and interactive advice.

Check if your university careers service offers psychometric tests. These can help with your self-analysis. Numeracy, literacy and diagrammatic reasoning tests can highlight your skills and strengths. They also provide a practice run for some employers' selection processes.

The test yourself section of this website also contains a range of online tests and self-assessment exercises.

Your university careers service may have books and exercises on self-assessment.

These activities should help you to produce a personal profile, which will be useful when you are making applications. You should be able to use your profile to provide evidence that you have the competences that employers require.

Your skills

What do employers want? The one thing they are all looking for is evidence of skills; in particular, the general skills used in a wide range of jobs.

Make a list of the skills you have developed during your studies. Here are some to get you started:

- working independently;
- planning time effectively;
- working under pressure and to deadlines;
- reading, analysing and synthesising vast amounts of material;
- solving problems;

- thinking originally and imaginatively;
- taking the initiative;
- articulating ideas and thoughts orally and in writing;
- adapting to different circumstances;
- presenting information in various ways (seminar papers, examination questions, group discussions, projects or presentations, laboratory reports).
- In your leisure time and vacations you will have added other skills/experience to your portfolio through jobs or work experience:
- organisational skills;
- ability to take responsibility for self and others;
- knowledge of the world of work;
- willingness to care/empathise;
- motivating others;
- improved communication skills;
- how to work in a team;
- ability to deal with difficult situations.

Do not overlook hobbies and interests, voluntary work or community involvement – they can provide evidence of your abilities. It is important to start thinking about yourself in this way because employers will.

If you are a mature graduate or job changer, or have been made redundant, you will probably have more evidence of relevant skills and experience to draw on. Present this in a positive way that an employer will value. It is easy to take your skills and experience for granted. Banish words like 'only' and 'just' from your vocabulary

Avoid the Resume Mistakes 8 tips.

1. *No clear focus.* Your résumé should show a clear match between your skills and experience and the job's requirements. Why are you the best person for this particular position?
2. *Dutifully dull.* A solid résumé is a tool to market yourself. Avoid phrases like "responsibilities included" or "duties included." Your résumé should be an declaration of your major accomplishments.
3. *Badly structured.* Information on a résumé should be listed in order of importance to the reader. Don't ask employers to wade through your hobbies first. Dates of employment are not as important as job titles. Education should be emphasized if you are freshly out of school and have little work experience; otherwise, put it at the end.
4. *Important skills buried.* Don't forget to bullet the important skills that make you a standout in your field. Your objective is to play up the value that you will bring to a prospective employer. Emphasize how you will add worth to the company, not the reason you want the job. Employers are looking for someone to enhance the organization, not their own résumé.
5. *Monotonous.* Try to stay away from the cookie-cutter résumé templates that employers see constantly. Show a little imagination when writing and designing your résumé. But don't overdo it.
6. *One typo too many.* Your résumé is your one chance to make a first impression. A typo or misspelled word can lead an employer to believe that you would not be a careful, detail-oriented employee. Spell-check software is not enough, since sentences like "Thank you for your patients" would get the thumbs up. Ask several people to proofread your résumé to be sure that it is free of typos and grammatical errors.
7. *True picture.* Everyone wants to present his or her work experience in the most attractive light, but information contained on your résumé must be true and accurate. Whether you're simply inflating past accomplishments or coming up with complete fabrications, lying is simply a bad idea.
8. *Skips the extras.* A common mistake is neglecting to mention any extra education, training, volunteer work, awards, or recognitions that might pertain to your particular job area or industry. Many employers view such "extracurricular activities" as testament to a well-rounded employee, so leverage such things as assets to distinguish your résumé from the hordes of others out there.

CHAPTER - 6

COVER LETTER

"A cover letter expresses your interest in and qualifications for a position to a prospective employer"

Job searching is a game. **"This is a must read for anyone looking for that extra edge in obtaining that all-important interview."** When applying for a job or submitting a resume blindly to a company, you should always include a cover letter, whether by mail or e-mail.

Jobseekers oftentimes underestimate the value a well-written and unique cover letter brings to their career package. The cover letters serves as an introducer, and if the introduction isn't done properly, the jobseeker has ruined yet another chance at a great job ... plus, he has laid the foundation for a longer job-search.

An effective cover letter should explain the reasons for your interest in the organization and in the job you are applying for.

- Your cover letter should introduce the main points of your resume.
- It should also help you to "sell" your qualifications to the prospective employer.
- Address your letter to a specific person, ideally to the person who will interview you.

- Look for the person's name in company publications, or phone the organization and ask for the person's name or for the personnel manager

Your cover letter tells an employer a lot about you, good or bad. Think of it as a sales pitch. It's primary purpose is to show why your skills and background are a perfect match for the position for which you're applying. It is not the place to present all of your experience, that should already be showcased in your resume.

As your first opportunity to make a great impression, a well-written letter shows that you are serious about your job search. Highlight one or two of your skills or accomplishments that show that you are the right person for this position.

While there is no set format or template, here are some more tips for creating a letter that employers will read:

Keep it brief. Cover letters rarely need to be longer than one page. You can usually sum it up in about four paragraphs:

Personalize. Avoid generic greetings such as "To Whom It May Concern" or "Dear Sir or Madam". Address your letter to a specific person, and make sure the spelling is correct.

Sell your skills. Don't just rehash your resume. Highlight the skills that are most relevant. Illustrate how they relate to the position.

Clarity is key. Be very direct; write clearly and concisely. Don't make the reader have to work to figure out why you're writing or speculate at how your skills match the position.

Be proactive. State how you can be reached and give specific information about your plans for follow-up. Once you've said it, do it; follow through.

Review, review, review. Always take the time to review your letter. Double-check for typos; don't rely on spell-check. If you have time, ask a friend or colleague to look it over as well. Make your changes and review again.

Introductory Paragraph

Your first paragraph should

- Get the reader's attention, stimulate interest, and be appropriate for the job you are seeking.

- Make your goal clear to readers.
- Preview the rest of your letter. Highlight the qualifications you will discuss throughout the letter.

Goals of the Body Paragraphs
- Highlight your strongest qualifications for the position for which you are applying.
- Demonstrate how these qualifications will benefit the employer.
- Refer employers to your enclosed resume

Detailing Your Experience
- Show (don't tell) employers your qualifications
- Include specific, credible examples of your qualifications for the position.
- Use numbers, names of equipment you've used, or features of a project that may apply to the job you want.

Using Active Language

Don'ts	Do's
Don't be vague in your descriptions.	Use concrete words to describe your experience.
Don't use weak verbs such as endeavored, tried, hoped, and attempted.	Use present tense to discuss current activities and past tense for previous job duties or accomplishments.
Don't use sexist language such as chairman and manpower.	Be as specific as possible in descriptions; list dollar amounts and figures when you can.

Organizing Your Letter
- In general, cover letters should be no longer than one typed page.
- Organize your body paragraphs to emphasize your strongest and most relevant qualifications. Only include the two or three strongest qualifications from your resume.
- Make it easy for readers to scan your letter by beginning each paragraph with a topic sentence

Format Sample Cover Letter - Programmer Analyst

Your Name
Your Address
Your City, State, Zip Code
Your Phone Number
Your Email
Company Name
Address
City, State, Zip Code

Dear HR Manager:

This letter is to express my interest in discussing the Senior Programmer Analyst position posted on the Company web site. The opportunity presented in this listing is very appealing, and I believe that my strong technical experience and education will make me a very competitive candidate for this position.

The key strengths that I possess for success in this position include but are not limited to the following:

- I have successfully designed, developed, and supported live use applications
- I am a self-starter
- Eager to learn new things
- Strive for continued excellence
- Provide exceptional contributions to customer service for all customers.

With a MS degree in Information Systems Management I have a full understanding of the full life cycle of a software development project.

I also have experience in learning and excelling at new technologies as needed. My experience includes but is not limited to:

- Customer service and support
- Programming both new applications and maintenance work
- Problem isolation and analysis
- Software quality testing
- Application and requirement analysis
- Process improvement and documentation

I am hereby enclosing my resume for your kind perusal.

Thank you for your time and consideration. I look forward to speaking with you about this employment opportunity.

Sincerely,
Your Name with Signature.

Sir/Madam,

I am a B.E/ B.Tech in XXXXXXXX-(*specify your branch*) with an aggregate of 85%. I will be much pleased (include the core of Cover Letter here). Here by I am sending / attaching a copy of my resume for your kind reference.

Core part of a Cover Letter.
- To work in a globally competitive environment on challenging assignments that shall yield the twin benefits of the job satisfaction and a steady-paced professional growth.
- To work efficiently and effectively as well as grow with a prestigious organization in field of production, maintenance, and designing. So as to achieve self realization and accomplishment of organizational goals.
- Seeking a challenging and satisfying career in Web Application Development environment.
- To work in a creative and challenging environment using cutting edge technologies where i could constantly learn and successfully deliver solutions to problems.
- To develop my career as a Software Engineer where I will be a valuable team member, contributing quality ideas and work for an organization where there is an ample scope for individual as well as organization growth in Software Design and Development.
- To be an excellent software professional and move into higher technology areas which provide an environment to improve my technical and analytical abilities.
- To be in a position in a result oriented company that seeks an ambitious and career conscious person where acquired skills and education will be utilized towards continuous growth and advancement.

Expecting a Favorable Reply,

Sincerely,

Your cover letter is your first (and best) chance to make a good impression! The cover letter gives you an opportunity to stand out from the dozens or maybe hundreds of other people who are applying for the same position as you are.

CHAPTER - 7

PROBLEM SOLVING SKILLS

The intuitive mind is a sacred gift and the rational mind is a faithful servant. We have created a society that honors the servant and has forgotten the gift.

—*Albert Einstein*

Problem Solving Skills

Reports are fact of life in today's business. In the high context culture values and attitudes seem to prompt us to write reports. We analyze the pros and cons of problems, studying alternatives and assessing facts, figures and details. We pride ourselves on being practical and logical. We solve problems by applying scientific procedures.

> "I have already explained to you that what is out of the common is usually a guide rather than a hindrance. In solving a problem of this sort, the grand thing is to be able to reason backward. That is a very useful accomplishment, and a very easy one, but people do not practise it much. In the everyday affairs of life it is more useful to reason forward, and so the other comes to be neglected. There are fifty who can reason synthetically for one who can reason analytically." [in A Study in Scarlet, 1887] *Sherlock Holmes*

Each researcher has a unique report to write, in spite of the seemingly endless rules and conventions you may feel surrounded by as you begin the task. Our aim is to support you in this task.

Research Writing Skills invites you to journey and browse as an independent learner through an orderly maze of information that can be entered from one of many points, depending on your need at the time.

You will discover in this set of materials a number of steps and processes, as well as suggestions and information, that will help you to construct your thesis as an entity made up of interlocking parts. At each step you are building on what you already have or can do, in order to move towards an envisaged end point. We hope that you will use these frameworks to devise and consolidate an approach of your own to writing your report. Each part can be surprisingly manageable when carefully structured to follow certain paths of logic and good communication.

This book introduces the report writing process and discusses methods of collecting and documenting data.

Communicating results is a crucial aspect of doing research. Through such communication other people can learn about and benefit from the findings. Often such communication includes a written document known as a *Technical Report*.

Technical report and proposal writing

Reports play an important part in the life of a professional engineer: they are a link between the writer and colleagues and clients world-wide. Engineers are often judged by the quality of their reports; a poorly composed document will not reflect your technical expertise or the reputation of your organization. The *Technical Report (TR)* is a common  written form through which computer scientist communicate their findings. Each TR should have a focused topic that is developed logically along some clearly identified perspective. The major components of a TR are title, author information, date, keywords, informative abstract, body, acknowledgments, references, and appendices. Typically, the body is organized into four sections: motivation, methods, results, and discussion.

There's no reason why technical writing shouldn't be lively and interesting. The real challenge is to express complex ideas simply. Too often technical writing has a flat style making documents difficult and tedious to read. As in all good writing, you should put across your message in clear English and avoid complex words, acronyms, jargon and passive verbs. You should also keep your average sentence length low. The real challenge in technical writing is to express complex ideas simply.

What is report?

An orderly, objective message used to convey information from one organisational area to another or from one institution to another. Reports communicate information which has been compiled as a result of research and analysis of data and of issues. Reports can cover a wide range of topics, but usually focus on transmitting information with a clear purpose, to a specific audience. Good reports are documents that are accurate, objective and complete. They should also be well-written, clearly structured and expressed in a way that holds the reader's attention and meets their expectations. The true value of the research may be assessed through a report since the written report may be the "only tangible product of hundreds of hours of work. Rightly or wrongly, the quality and worth of that work are judged by the quality of the written report - its clarity, organization and content" (Blake & Bly, 1993: 119). Often reports are structured in a way that reflects the information finding process and the writing up of the findings: that is, summary of the contents, introduction or background, methods, results, discussion, conclusion and/or recommendations. The inclusion of recommendations is one reason why reports are a common form of writing in industry, as the informed recommendations are useful for decision making.

The scope and style of reports varies widely. It depends on three key factors: the report's intended audience, the report's purpose and the type of information to be communicated; for example, technical reports communicate technical information, so the degree of technicality in the report will depend on the reader's familiarity and understanding of technical concepts.

In industry, technical reports are used to communicate technical information. This information assists in decision making: for example, in the purchase of equipment, or finding solutions to technical problems. An important consideration when preparing technical reports is the audience and purpose of the report: for example, to brief managers, to provide technical background information for lay people associated with the project, or to make recommendations to technical supervisors. These factors determine the degree of technicality of the language and concepts involved.

At university, technical report writing is a frequently used assignment format in faculties of engineering and in the applied sciences. This is because the assignment tasks require students to draw theory and real world situations together, and to present the information in a structured and accessible format; for example, engineering students may be asked to solve a design problem or investigate and evaluate the solutions to an environmental problem while Information Technology students might be asked to develop a program or an information management plan for a specific issue or company or to evaluate recent developments in the telecommunications industry. Learning how to report on technical information to others is an important component of technical studies.

Types of reports
1. Periodic Operating Reports.
2. Situational Reports
3. Investigative / Informational Reports.
4. Compliance Reports
5. Recommendation Reports
6. Yardstick Reports
7. Feasibility Reports
8. Research Studies.

Feasibility Reports
- Assess several alternatives
- using criteria
- and recommend the best alternative

Proposal

It is an offer to perform one (or more) of the following services:
- furnish goods or services
- research a subject
- provide a solution to a problem,

to persuade the reader to follow your proposal and/or apply for funding.

* It may be solicited or unsolicited.

Functions of reports

Informational Reports : Reports that present data without analysis or recommendations are primarily informational.

Analytical Reports : Reports that provide data, analysis and conclusions.

Progress Reports
Provide information about :
- progress achieved, and
- timetable for future work and completion

to

- identify possible problems, and
- make decisions about resource allocation

Parts of Progress report
- INTRODUCTION
  (explanation of the project)
- WORK TO DATE
  (accomplishments & problems)
- FUTURE WORK
- CONCLUSION
  (situation overall)

Writing that Works // Understand the type of technical report you are writing.

Technical reports come in all shapes and sizes, but they all share the same goal of communicating information clearly. Deciding what type of document you need to write is an important first step as it influences your approach.

Reporting Research Findings

These documents describe the work done to gather information in the laboratory or field. They can be simple recording or data or more thorough and include: the problem or issue examined, the method or equipment used, the data collected and the implications.

Simple Technical Information Report

This document explains a technical subject. It has no aim other than to make sure readers understand the topic clearly. For example, a technical report on a investing in the futures market would probably explain how the market evolved, how it works, the specialist terms used and so on. A simple technical report for information does not put forward a view on the merits of investing in the market or have recommendations.

Technical Specifications

Specifications typically consist of descriptions of the features, materials, uses and workings of new product. Good specifications concentrate on graphics, data and illustrations rather than written descriptions. Think of a patent application as a good example.

Technical Evaluation Reports

Evaluation reports, sometimes called feasibility reports, present technical information in a practical and logical way to decide whether something is possible. For example, a technical evaluation report into setting up an intranet site for a corporation would examine if this was possible, set out the steps needed and point out any problems. It does not recommend if the corporation should set up its own intranet site.

Technical Recommendation Reports

These reports lead to specific recommendations. It builds on the evaluation report and comes to specific recommendations to help the decision-maker adopt the best solution. Of course, some reports often have both the evaluation and recommendation reports rolled into one

Technical Manuals and Instructions

Here the emphasis is on using appliances, equipment or programs. The task here is to write step-by-step procedures anyone can understand and follow.

Organizing Your Report

Anatomy of a Report
- **Cover Page**
- **Title Page**
- **Letter of Transmittal**
- **Table of Contents**
- **Executive Summary**
- **Report Body**
- **Introduction**
- **Discussion**
- **Conclusions**
- **Recommendations**
- **Bibliography**

Title Page

Title ,Author's name,

Module Name & Number

Seminar Leader, Date of Submission.

Letter of Transmittal
- Background
- Summarize conclusions and recommendations
- Minor problems. Thank those who helped.
- Additional research necessary
- Thank the reader. Offer to answer questions

Table of Contents

Abstract/ Executive Summary

Table of Contents
1. Introduction   1
2. Discussion   2
3. Conclusion   3
4. Recommendations   4
5. Bibliography   5

Executive Summary
- A paragraph at the very beginning
- Describes the most important facts and conclusions
- Write it *last* (when you know what to summarize!)

Introduction
- Several paragraphs, describing
- Background
- Questions of interest
- Data you have worked with
  OK to repeat material from Executive Summary

Discussion / Analysis and Methods
- Interpret the data, presenting
- Graphic displays, statistical summary numbers, results
- The four basic activities: design, explore, estimate, test
- Explain as you go along

Conclusions and Summary
- Move back to the big picture

- Give closure
- Pull together all important thoughts you would like your readers to remember

Recommendations
- Suggestions for possible actions based on the research
- Recommendations to business community or other relevant groups as appropriate

Bibliography / Reference
- Note indicating material taken from an outside source
- Enough information so your audience can locate it
- Could be a footnote on the same page as the material
- Could all be gathered together in one section at the end

Appendix
- Supporting material
- Important enough to be included
- Not important enough to appear in the text of the paper
- It's there for the interested reader

If you don't organize your document well, readers may miss important information. It is up to you to present your information in a readable and well-organized way. You should offer informative summaries, clear instructions and a logical arrangement to let your readers pick and choose the parts they want to read. Isn't it easy to navigate and get the information you want quickly? As readers will not read from the opening page to the last page, good organization here is essential. This is just as true of a manual where readers need to find out how to fix a problem or a report where the reader wants to find the reason for a technical decision.

So it's a good idea to write down the sections and subsections you need to plan your document

Five Steps to Report Writing

1. Define the problem
2. Gather the necessary information
3. Analyze the information
4. Organize the information
5. Write the report

1. ***Introduction*** **:** The ability to write clear, concise reports is an asset to almost any professional. In this article I offer some general guidelines on report writing, focusing particularly on something I call the 'standard model'. This 'standard model' is a formalisation of the way that scientific reports have usually been written over the last fifty years or so. While the standard model has its detractors, and is often used inappropriately, it still has a lot to recommend it. I normally suggest to students who don't have much writing experience that they follow this model unless they have good reasons not to. In this article I will also try to explain *why* we recommend that reports are written in a particular way.

2. ***Fundamentals*** **:** The main purpose of a technical report is to convey information. The report should place as few hindrances as possible between the mind of the writer and the mind of the reader. A secondary function is to stimulate and entertain. There are people — a tiny minority — who can inform and entertain at the same time. If, like most people, you have to make a choice between the two, you should try to inform rather than to entertain. Of course, if you were writing a novel the priorities would be reversed; but in report writing it is the information that is paramount.

A good report needs careful planning. As part of the planning stage you should try to answer the following questions.

What is the report *about*? What are you trying to say? You should arrange things so that they key facts and conclusions are very accessible. Not everyone will read the whole report, so ensure that your message will get across even if a person only skims the document. I have been told — and tend to believe — that senior managers have an attention span of about four minutes. This suggests that if you are writing with these people as your audience, your report should start with a summary that can be read in a few minutes. In fact, this is a good idea whatever the audience.

Who are you writing for? It is simply impossible to write a technical document that will be equally easy for everybody to read: the level of explanation you need for an expert audience is totally different from that needed for readers who are unfamiliar with the subject. It is absolutely essential that you identify the potential readers — the professional group, not the individuals — before you start work. In the university environment your report will probably be read by lecturers. These people will have a good knowledge of their subject in general, but will probably not know much about the precise field of your report. You should always bear this in mind. If you are writing for computer scientists you don't need to explain, for example, what a modem is, nor the World-Wide Web, but you *will* need to explain what phase modulation is, and what 'CGI' stands for.

How long can the report be? It's difficult to predict in advance exactly how long a report will be, but you should be able to decide whether you will be writing 2,000 words or 20,000 words. It's generally harder to write a short report than a long one, because it requires much better organisation. In the university environment there may be official limitations on the size of the report.

3. ***The standard model :*** The 'standard model' of report writing is a style and structure that has been widely used in the western world for about 50 years. It is the reporting method that is usually taught in schools. Contrary to what we are taught in schools, however, it is *not* the only accepted way to write in science. Nevertheless, it is the way that most professional scientists and engineers choose to write. The main features of a report that follows the 'standard model' are as follows.

The first major section is an introduction; the last is a conclusion. The conclusion answers questions posed — explicitly or otherwise — in the introduction.

Factual material and measurements are kept completely separate from opinion and interpretation, often in different chapters or sections.

Formal, and rather impersonal, language is used.

The report usually refers quite extensively to the work of other individuals.

The sections of the report are numbered.

Most 'standard model' reports will contain some or all of the following sections, *usually in this order*. Each of these sections will be discussed in more detail below.

'Abstract' or 'summary'.

'Acknowledgements'.

'Introduction'.

'Objectives'.

'Theory'.

'Method' or 'methodology' or 'procedures'.

'Results'.

'Discussion' or 'interpretation'.

'Conclusion'.

'Recommendations'.

'References' and/or 'bibliography'.

'Appendices'.

A 'standard model' report will probably also contain a table of contents, a list of abbreviations and technical terms, and perhaps an index if the document is long.

Abstract or summary

An abstract or summary (they mean essentially the same thing) should contain a brief overview of the report, including its conclusions and recommendations if there are any. A good length for an abstract is 300 words; some scientific journals actually specify this number of words explicitly. The abstract of a scientific paper or report is considered to be capable of 'standing alone' and being published separately. For this reason the heading 'abstract' in a report is usually not numbered. Numbering usually starts with the introduction.

Introduction

The introduction sets out what the report is about, and what its role is in relation to other work in the field. If describing experiments, the introduction will usually summarise other related experiments, and show how the work to be described extends or supersedes these earlier studies. If the report is about development (e.g., software development) the introduction will often set out what the purpose of the development is, who will benefit, and how it will be used. If the report is a review, it will usually just state the scope of the report and the readership for which it is intended.

In most technical reports, the introduction will say something about the context of the report, that is, how the work it describes forms part of the overall body of work in that subject area. When describing an investigation, the introduction will usually state explicitly what the investigators set out to find.

My approach is to finish the introduction with a list of the questions I set out to answer, and give the answers to these questions in the conclusions. I like to be quite explicit about this, and even label the questions 'question 1', 'question 2', etc. Whether you do this or not, the reader should be able to look at the conclusion of your report and verify that you have found out what you claimed you would find out.

Objectives

This section, if present, states what the work being reported was expected to achieve, why it was undertaken, and at whose instigation. I usually prefer to put this information at the end of the introduction, but this is just a matter of taste.

Acknowledgements

It is polite to give a brief note of thanks to those people who have helped *directly* in the work the report describes. In a novel, the authors often thank their friends and family; most scientists and engineers consider it slightly pretentious to do this in a technical report. In the last few weeks I have read technical reports that acknowledged the invaluable assistance of the late Princess of Wales, Jesus, and the author's pet dog.

If the report is destined for publication, and describes work supported by a grant, the grant-awarding body may insist that it be acknowledged. It seems reasonable to me to do this.

Theory

The theory section, if used, describes any background theory needed for the reader to understand the report. Such a section is usually found only in reports that use mathematics that the typical reader cannot be expected to know in advance.

Method

In the 'method' section you should describe the way the work was carried out, what equipment you used, and any particular problems that had to be overcome. If the report is describing a survey, you should say how you chose your subjects, how you checked for bias, and how you analysed the results.

Results

In the standard model, results are usually given as plainly as possible, and without any comment. It is often difficult to know how much data to put into this section. My feeling is that you should include enough data to enable to reader to be confident that you have done what you said you would do, and that your conclusions will be trustworthy. This certainly does not mean that you should include reams of print-outs and copies of questionnaire returns. I try to summarise the results into a few tables and graphs.

Most readers that are used to reading scientific reports will become uncomfortable if you call a section 'results' and put anything in it apart from plain results.

Discussion

In this section the author provides an interpretation of the results, compares them with other published findings — if there are any — and points out any potential shortcomings in the work.

The 'discussion' section of a traditional report is the place where the author is allowed to be less objective than usual. In this section it is acceptable to mention opinions, and speculate slightly about the significance of the work.

In particular, if your findings are unusual, or very much at odds with other people's conclusions, you should explain why you think this might be. Otherwise the reader will probably assume you have just made a mistake.

Conclusion

The conclusion gives the overall findings of the study. It is important to realise that 'conclusion' does *not* just mean 'the last bit of the report'. Your conclusions should really be statements that can be concluded from the rest of the work. A conclusion is not a summary. (You can include a summary as well, if you like). When I mark students' reports, one of the questions I ask about them is 'do the conclusions follow from the body of the report?'

Recommendations

In this section the author normally includes any advice he or she wishes to offer the reader. If the report is about making some sort of business decision, the appropriate course of action will usually be recommended here. Some people use the recommendations sections for suggestions of further work, which seems reasonable to me.

References and bibliography

The purpose of citing references is to allow the reader to follow up your work, and perhaps check that the conclusions you draw really follow from the sources you cite. References are not, as many students appear to think, a method for convincing the examiner that you have read a lot. You should give enough detail that if the reader wanted to follow up your references, he or she would be able to do so. For books, you should give the authors, year, edition (if there's more than one), publisher's name and publisher's location. For articles in journals give the authors, year, name of the publication, volume and page numbers. If you can't give all these details, you probably don't have a proper reference.

The rise in Web-based publishing has created its own citation problems. The same basic principle applies, however, as it does to citing printed works: the citation must be sufficient to allow the reader to follow up the reference. If possible, you should cite a URL that will take the reader directly to the document you cite. Giving the URL for a 'home' or 'welcome' page is generally not helpful. As a matter of good style, you should give the names of the authors and the publication date, if you are able to determine them.

Although it is not peculiar to Web-based publication, authors should be aware of the problem that not all references have equal weight. References to articles in peer-reviewed journals will be more convincing than references to non-reviewed sources. Since anyone can publish anything on a Web site, there is a real risk of citing something that is not very authoritative.

Many students seem not to know the difference between 'references' and 'bibliography'. The bibliography is the set of publications that the authors referred to *in a general sense* in writing the report or carrying out the work it describes. These publications will not usually be cited explicitly in the text. References, on the other hand, are given in support of some specific assertion, and are always mentioned explicitly in the text. Normally this citation would be given after the statement the author wants to support. A common method is to give the authors and year in the text, e.g, (Bloggs, 1995), and the full details at the end of the report or in a footnote.

In scientific writing, if you make any statement that is not one of plain fact or measurement, you *must* justify it, or refer the reader to another publication where it is justified. The making of unjustified assertions is probably the single most common criticism leveled at students' writing.

If you use another person's words directly, you *must* be clear about this and give a full reference. If you use more than a few words, or a picture, or results, you should seek the author's permission first, and state in your report that you obtained such permission. If you don't do this you're probably breaking the law, as well as being unprofessional.

Appendices

The appendices are where the author will usually place any material that is not directly relevant to the report, and will only be read by small number of people. I usually use appendices for mathematical proofs, electrical circuit diagrams and sections of computer programs.

Numbering and structure

It is common to number each section of the report. Usually numbering starts at the introduction, which has number '1', and continues until the references. Because they are in a sense independent of the body of the report, the abstract and references are not usually numbered. Most people number sub-sections as well. So, for example, in section one, sub-section two would be numbered '1.2'. Other people prefer to use numbers and letters, e.g., 1A, 1B... This is fine as well. The advantage of using a hierarchical numbering scheme like this is that it helps to orient the reader. It allows the most important section divisions to be identified at a glance.

When should you use the standard model?

Writers of technical reports should use the standard model, or something close to it, unless there is a sound reason not to. Why? First, and most important, its use is so widespread that the reader will know exactly what to expect in each section. Moreover, if the reader needs to refer to your report quickly he or she will know immediately which section to turn to. Second, it is well 'signposted'; even people who are not familiar with this type of report will find the clear section divisions useful in their understanding. Third, the rigid organisation of the report will help the novice writer organise his or her thoughts when writing.

There are times when the standard model will be a hindrance, rather than a help. In these cases you should cheerfully abandon it and adopt something else. In particular, you don't need to include all the sections. A 'results' section, for example, is only useful if you are reporting results or measurements.

4. *Alternatives to the standard model*

Here are a few suggestions of other ways to organise a technical report.

The 'segmented' standard model

If a report describes a set of investigations with a common purpose, but different methodologies, it can be rather difficult to use the standard model, even if each individual investigation could be reported that way. In this case it is quite useful to give each experiment its own 'segment', with a 'method' and 'results' section, but use single overall 'introduction' and 'discussion' sections. In the 'segments', one does not necessarily need to use explicit sub-sections for method and results, as long as the reader is clear where the boundaries are.

The 'assertion' model

This is quite unusual in a report (it is widely used in presentations and posters) but in some circumstances it can be very effective. In this type of report, rather than using very passive section titles like 'Introduction', the author uses very active, direct statements, like 'the new protocol improves communications efficiency by 23%'. The headings together make up a summary of the report. Of course, if you make an assertion you then have to go on to defend it. The great advantage of this type of presentation is that the reader can get an overall idea of what the report says simply by reading the headings at the top of each section.

The 'conclusion first' model

In this type of report, the conclusions are presented towards the beginning, perhaps directly after the introduction. In my opinion one should re-state or summarise the conclusions at the end as well, otherwise the report ends abruptly. The advantage of placing the conclusion at the beginning is that it is more likely to be read. It also allows the reader to have the conclusions in mind while reading the rest of the report. I don't use this method myself; I prefer to put a short summary of the conclusions in the abstract.

The 'topic' model

In this type of report, each section of the report is on a particular topic or subject, but there will probably be a common introduction and conclusion. This structure is appropriate for review or instructional articles, but is probably not very useful for scientific reports. The problem here is that it does not lend itself to the division between methodology, results and interpretation that most readers will expect.

5. *Language, style and presentation*

If your message is one of profound importance, it will be communicated rapidly even if presented badly. On the whole, however, few scientific and technical reports contain ground-breaking findings. In this case the author must pay more attention to issues of communication to encourage people to read the report.

Grammar and spelling

Most academics and scientists, and many businesspeople, are relatively selective about grammar and spelling. This is probably because such people read a great deal, and have learned to extract as much information from a document as possible in a limited time. This is only possible if everyone follows very similar standards of grammar and spelling..

If your grammar and spelling are not particularly good, it is vital that you have your work read by someone else before you decide that it's finished. At the very least you should get a printed copy of your document and check it very thoroughly yourself.

Style

Most technical documents are written in a rather formal style. Some readers get upset when they have to read reports that are written informally. For example, if the author adopts a impersonal, formal style (using phrases like 'at this point the operator should click on the button labelled "start"...') and suddenly switches to an informal, personal form ('now you should click on "start"...'), it can be very confusing.

The use of passive-voice expressions has probably derived from authors' attempts to give the impression of impartiality when reporting scientific findings. I don't think anyone will be fooled into thinking than if you sound impartial, you are impartial. But that's just my opinion.

In general, I think appropriate humour is fine in a technical report. The problem is this: if your report is about, say, theorem proving methods, what sort of humour is likely to be appropriate? Many attempted jokes detract badly from the message the author wants to convey. Nevertheless, occasionally it works.

On the whole you should probably not write the way you speak, for two reasons. First, you probably use colloquial and ungrammatical expressions in your speech that the reader will not understand (I'm sure I do). The reader cannot stop you and ask for an explanation. Second, in writing you don't have access to the differences in emphasis and tone of voice that help spoken communication. As you have to rely entirely on the words themselves, you need to choose them with some care.

Presentation

Good presentation is, less important than sound technical content. However, that does not mean that it is unimportant: the decision about how much time a potential reader is prepared to spend looking at your report will be based to a large extent on the first impression made by the presentation.

The final part of report preparation is usually binding. It doesn't cost very much to have a report spiral-bound, and it will be much easier to read than if it is stapled or ring-bound.

Presentation

For technical reports required as part of an assessment, the following presentation guidelines are recommended;

Script	The report must be printed single sided on white A4 paper. Hand written or dot-matrix printed reports are not acceptable.
Margins	All four margins must be at least 2.54 cm
Page numbers	Do not number the title, summary or contents pages. Number all other pages consecutively starting at 1
Binding	A single staple in the top left corner or 3 staples spaced down the left hand margin. For longer reports (e.g. year 3 project report) binders may be used.

6. *Visual material*

Very few technical reports con sists only of text; it is usual to include graphs, photographs, or charts as well. Label everything. All charts and graphs should have a caption and perhaps a number ('figure 1'). Check that when you refer to figures in the text, these references are correct. It commonly happens that people add or remove figures, then forget to update all the cross-references.

Diagrams, graphs, tables and mathematics

It is often the case that technical information is most concisely and clearly conveyed by means other than words. Imagine how you would describe an electrical circuit layout using words rather than a circuit diagram. Here are some simple guidelines;

Diagrams	Keep them simple. Draw them specifically for the report. Put small diagrams after the text reference and as close as possible to it. Think about where to place large diagrams.
Graphs	For detailed guidance on graph plotting, see the 'guide to laboratory report writing'
Tables	Is a table the best way to present your information? Consider graphs, bar charts or pie charts.
	Dependent tables (small) can be placed within the text, even as part of a sentence.
	Independent tables (larger) are separated from the text with table numbers and captions. Position them as close as possible to the text reference. Complicated tables should go in an appendix.
Mathematics	Only use mathematics where it is the most efficient way to convey the information. Longer mathematical arguments, if they are really necessary, should go into an appendix. You will be provided with lecture handouts on the correct layout for mathematics.

References to diagrams, graphs, tables and equations

- In the main text you must always refer to any diagram, graph or table which you use.
- Label diagrams and graphs as follows; Figure 1.2 Graph of energy output as a function of wave height. In this example, the second diagram in section 1 would be referred to by "...see figure 1.2..."
- Label tables in a similar fashion;

  Table 1 Performance specifications of a range of commercially available GaAsFET devices

In this example, the first table in section 3 might be referred to by "...with reference to the performance specifications provided in Table 3.1..."

Number equations as follows;

$$F(dB) = 10 \times \log_{10}(F) \quad (3.6)$$

In this example, the sixth equation in section 3 might be referred to by "...noise figure in decibels as given by eqn (3.6)..."

If you prepare graphs in colour, then print them on a monochrome printer, they may become unreadable. For example, it will not be possible to distinguish between a line that was originally back and one that was blue. Some computer software automatically converts graphs to use dotted and dashed lines on a printer, but most does not.

Photographs do not usually photocopy very well. You may need to get extra prints made of photographs so that you can include prints with each copy of the report.

Unlike in an advertising or promotional brochure, colour presentation is not usually worth the extra effort in a technical document (except in certain subjects, like computer graphics and multimedia). It's worth checking this before starting work on the report.

Computer software that is designed for producing slide presentations will often not use sensible type sizes when used for producing diagrams for printing on paper. A good size for text labels on a diagram is 12-14 points.

7. *Things to avoid*

Avoid clichés and stock phrases. *Clichés* are phrases that were probably witty and stylish when introduced, but their very appeal has made them so over-used that they are likely to annoy the reader. They will be quite likely to have seen the same cliché used several times that day. Here are some particularly common examples: 'at the end of the day...', 'explore every avenue', 'not to put too fine a point on it...', 'going foward, we will...'

Hints and Tips
- **Think about your audience**
- **Keep it brief**
- Select only the most important results, graphs, conclusions
- Put others in the Appendix if they must be there at all
- **Make it clear**
- Use straightforward language

Example : Avoid jargon let the language be simple and easy to read. Suppose you have to explain how the cooling mechanism in a warehouse works. You may have to assume the expert and the nonexpert audiences both understand common terms such as **ring seal, stop value, thermostat**. But you may need to explain more complex terms, such as **coolant temperature matrix**, even if expert readers know the terms . Remember, readers can usually handle a few specialist words or terms if the writing style is concise and easy to read.
- Orient your reader
- No need for suspense - put important results early!
- **Look it over**

- Pretend you *are* your audience, not the analyst
- Try to forget the details you know about the project
- Can you learn easily from the report

Poor Technical Writing	Concise and Easy to Read
The 15ATS series toggle switches, in excess of 200 in total, were subject to the extreme of temperatures caused by being in close proximity to the furnace. This in turn caused heat failure as the expansion of metal caused a fault whereby the metal connection fused. The heat of the furnace has to be over 600 degrees Fahrenheit before this effect takes place.	Over 200 automatic toggle switches fused when the keypad melted as the furnace temperature rose to over 600 degrees Fahrenheit

What to Write First? Next? Last?
- Do the analysis first
- Accumulate lots of material
- Select the most important results; choose carefully
- Make an outline
- Analysis and Methods section; Conclusion
- Write a paragraph for each line of your outline
- Then decide what to place in Appendix, choose references
- Front material is easiest to write *last*
- Executive Summary, Introduction are best written once you know what you are summarizing and introducing
- Read and revise rough draft; ask a friend to help

Stock phrases are slightly different from clichés; they are phrases that writers in a particular discipline tend to use too often, not because they read well, but because they get used to reading them. Particular examples include 'at this point in time...', 'in the opinion of the author...' The problem with these phrases is that often they add nothing at all the the content, or could be replaced by a single word. For example 'at this point in time...' can usefully be replaced by 'now...'

Avoid giving too much data. I favour including only a summary of experimental data in a report.

The report layout

The appearance of a report is no less important than its content. An attractive, clearly organised report stands a better chance of being read. Use a standard, 12pt, font, such as Times New Roman, for the main text. Use different font sizes, bold, italic and underline where appropriate but not to excess.

Avoid computer program listings and long mathematical proofs. It is unlikely that anyone will want to read them, and anyone who does want to can ask you for a copy later.

8. *General guidelines*

Finally, here are a few general suggestions, in no particular order.

Decide what you want to say, then say it. It is very difficult to think about what conclusions to draw from your investigation, for example, at the same time as writing these conclusions. When you come to write a report, you should be in a position to think only about reporting, not about investigation or data interpretation.

Before you write very much, check whether there are standards you are required to conform to. As a student you may find that your place of study has quite detailed rules about report presentation. At PhD level it almost certainly will. Some institutions specify exactly which typefaces to use for various levels of heading, and so on. You'll have to do all the formatting and layout yourself, according to the journal's rules. For most journals, however, you'll be expected to provide plain text — no layout or formatting — and the figures on separate pages. I mention this because there's no point spending time on getting the flow of text around your figures exactly right, when you'll end up putting them on separate pages.

A shorter report is a better report. If you can say the same in 2000 words as in 5000, then it's better to write 2000 words. Be ruthless: edit your work thoroughly after writing.

People find it hard to be critical of their own work. I suggest that you regard everything you write as a draft, until it has been read by at least one other person. That other person need not be an expert in the subject, in fact it is often better if you choose someone who is not an expert.

It's usually better not to edit your document *at all* until you have written the whole thing, at least to first-draft standard.

Writing good reports is difficult, and usually takes longer than the author anticipates. If possible, allow yourself twice as much time as you first think you'll need.

Bibliography

There are many good books on the subject of technical writing, but, in my opinion, none of these are written by or for computer scientists.

- Davies J.W. *Communication for Engineering Students* (Longman 1996)
- van Emden J. *Effective communication for Science and Technology* (Palgrave 2001)
- King LS (1978) *Why not say it clearly?* (Boston: Little, Brown and Company)
- Pfeiffer W.S. *Pocket Guide to Technical Writing* (Prentice Hall 1998)

Common Mistakes to Avoid

Adhere carefully to the following guidelines:

1. In the introduction of your report, clearly identify a focused well-defined question. Answer this question in the rest of your report.
2. Analyze and interpret your data, and discuss the significance and limitations of your findings. Do not simply report your data.
3. Be sure that your technical report is complete in the sense that it has each of the following components: descriptive title, author name and affiliation, date, informative abstract, list of keywords, body, acknowledgments, and references.

In your abstract, specifically and concretely state your findings; do not vaguely describe what you set out to do. Your abstract should summarize, not introduce. Do not begin your abstract with the hackneyed phrase "This paper."

Section	Details
Title page	Must include the title of the report. Reports for assessment, where the word length has been specified, will often also require the summary word count and the main text word count
Summary	A summary of the whole report including important features, results and conclusions
Contents	Numbers and lists all section and subsection headings with page numbers
Introduction	States the objectives of the report and comments on the way the topic of the report is to be treated. Leads straight into the report itself. Must not be a copy of the introduction in a lab handout.
The sections which make up the body of the report	Divided into numbered and headed sections. These sections separate the different main ideas in a logical order.
Conclusions	A short, logical summing up of the theme(s) developed in the main text.
References	Details of published sources of material referred to or quoted in the text (including any lecture notes and URL addresses of any websites used.
Bibliography	Other published sources of material, including websites, not referred to in the text but useful for background or further reading.
Acknowledgements	List of people who helped you research or prepare the report, including your proofreaders.
Appendices (if appropriate)	Any further material which is essential for full understanding of your report (e.g. large scale diagrams, computer code, raw data, specifications) but not required by a casual reader.

CHAPTER - 8

CORRESPONDENCE TECHNIQUES

> **Improve writing skills**
> **5 Great Tips to Effective Letter Writing**
>
> Many people might wonder the need for letter writing in a world dominated by emails. If you wish to streamline your communication, never ignore the power of a well constructed letter. An email cannot achieve the impact that a well written letter can generate. Whether it is business, sales, cover or personal letter, you can master it by learning some simple tips.
>
> 1. The content of a letter should be planned well. To streamline your communication, make a draft of your letter. This will help in communicating effectively. Make sure that all the points have been detailed and check your letter for readability. Rephrase those sentences that can be misunderstood. Check the spelling, especially, the name of the receiver. Another key aspect is the consistency in the spelling of names. To be on the safer side, it is always wise to prepare a draft of business, sales and cover letters.
>
> 2. Use of language. For business letters, always use formal language. Sales letters need to attract potential customers. So they can be informal with catchy headlines. But when the sales letter talks about guarantee, delivery and other core issues, use a formal tone. Cover letters should always be written in formal language. Maximum flexibility with language can be shown in a personal letter. Depending upon your relationship, you can choose a formal or informal language. To streamline your communication, you should learn the art of selecting the appropriate tone for your letter.

3. Your letter might be intended for several people. This does not mean that it should not have a personal touch. Always write a business or sales letter like writing to a single person. A personal touch in your sales letter or newsletter will make the reader feel more comfortable. The reader should never feel like reading a brochure. The letter should have the effect of a personal conversation.

4. One of the best methods to streamline your communication is to make effective use of all modern day writing techniques. Use headlines to indicate the subject matter. Make use of bullets to detail important points. Use simple language. If a scientific term is used explain it in parentheses. You can make use of italics, bolding and underling in the letter. You can also create a template for your letter.

5. Brevity. Today, people do not have time to spend on reading long letters. Make your point in least number of words. Never deviate from the core subject. Unnecessary deviations from the subject can do more harm than good. Sometimes the reader might totally ignore the letter.

Letters are an important tool of communication. Remember, they can also become documental evidences. Your success in the modern day world depends on how effectively you are able to streamline your communication.

Influence through letters - Business Letters

The style and manner of writing business letters says a lot about the individual and their organisation. Many people lack confidence in their letter writing, or would like to improve their skills in this area. Letters are probably the most common form of communication used by housing organizations, and it is therefore vital that they carry the right message: both in terms of information communicated as well as the image presented. It is essential to understand that writing for a business context or audience can be distinctly different than writing in the humanities, social sciences, or other academic disciplines. Writing for business should be crisp and succinct.

In most cases, the business letter will be the first impression that you make on someone. For this reason it is important that you are diligent in your task of writing an effective business document. Business writing varies from the chatty, conversational style often found in email messages to a familiar co-worker, to the more formal, legalistic style found in contracts. In the majority of memos, email messages, and letters, a style between these two extremes is appropriate. Always remember, writing that is too formal can alienate readers, and an overly obvious attempt to be causal and informal may strike the reader as insincere or unprofessional. In business writing, as in all writing, knowing your audience is critical.

> A 1997 study of English teachers by Dr. Bernard Lamb of London University revealed that:
>
> "In a writing test, English teachers "missed out apostrophes, commas and hyphens and made numerous other punctuation and grammatical errors"
>
> in a survey "only half the English teachers explicitly taught spelling and grammar . . ." that documents sent out to schools by the Department of Education and Employment "were littered with mistakes."
>
> If some English teachers exhibit these deficiencies in their knowledge of the language, how confident can you be of those they taught - your staff?

Parts of a business letter

Date

The date line is used to indicate the date the letter was written For example: June 11, 2001.) Write out the month, day and year two inches from the top of the page. Depending which format you are using for your letter, either left justify the date or center it horizontally.

Sender's Address

Including the address of the sender is optional. If you choose to include it, place the address one line below the date. Do not write the sender's name or title, as it is included in the letter's closing. Include only the street address, city and zip code. Another option is to include the sender's address directly after the closing signature.

Inside Address

The inside address is the recipient's address. It is always best to write to a specific individual at the firm to which you are writing. If you do not have the person's name, do some research by calling the company or speaking with employees from the company. Include a personal title such as Ms., Mrs., Mr., or Dr. Follow a woman's preference in being addressed as Miss, Mrs., or Ms. If you are unsure of a woman's preference in being addressed, use Ms. If there is a possibility that the person to whom you are writing is a Dr. or has some other title, use that title. To write the address, use the U.S. Post Office Format. For international addresses, type the name of the country in all-capital letters on the last line. The inside address begins one line below the sender's address or one inch below the date. It should be left justified, no matter which format you are using.

Salutation

Use the same name as the inside address, including the personal title. If you know the person and typically address them by their first name, it is acceptable to use only the first name in the salutation (i.e., Dear Lucy:). In all other cases, however, use the personal title and full name followed by a colon. Leave one line blank after the salutation.

If you don't know a reader's gender, use a nonsexist salutation, such as "To Whom it May Concern." It is also acceptable to use the full name in a salutation if you cannot determine gender. For example, you might write *Dear Harry Hermon:*

Body

For block and modified block formats, single space and left justify each paragraph within the body of the letter. Leave a blank line between each paragraph. When writing a business letter, be careful to remember that conciseness is very important. In the first paragraph, consider a friendly opening and then a statement of the main point. The next paragraph should begin justifying the importance of the main point. In the next few paragraphs, continue justification with background information and supporting details. The closing paragraph should restate the purpose of the letter and, in some cases, request some type of action.

Closing

The closing begins at the same horizontal point as your date and one line after the last body paragraph. Capitalize the first word only (i.e., Thank you) and leave four lines between the closing and the sender's name for a signature. If a colon follows the salutation, a comma should follow the closing; otherwise, there is no punctuation after the closing.

Enclosures

If you have enclosed any documents along with the letter, such as a resume, you indicate this simply by typing Enclosures one line below the closing. As an option, you may list the name of each document you are including in the envelope.

When writing business letters, you must pay special attention to the format and font used. The most common layout of a business letter is known as block format. Using this format, the entire letter is left justified and single spaced except for a double space between paragraphs. Another widely utilized format is known as modified block format. In this type, the body of the letter is left justified and single-spaced. However, the date and closing are in alignment in the center of the page. The final, and least used, style is semi-block. It is much like the modified block style except that each paragraph is indented instead of left justified.

The generally accepted font is Times New Roman, size 12, although other fonts such as Arial may be used. When choosing a font, always consider your audience. If you are writing to a conservative company, you may want to use Times New Roman. As far as punctuation after the salutation and closing is concerned, the standard is to use a colon after the salutation (never a comma) and a comma after the closing. There is also a less accepted format, known as open punctuation, in which punctuation is excluded after the salutation and the closing.

Block format
January 16, 2007
5 Hill Street
Madison, Wisconsin 53700
Ms. Helen Jones
President
Jones, Jones & Jones
23 International Lane
Boston, Massachusetts 01234
Dear Ms. Jones:
The first paragraph of a typical business letter is used to state the main point of the letter. Begin with a friendly opening; then quickly transition into the purpose of your letter. Use a couple of sentences to explain the purpose, but do not go in to detail until the next paragraph.

Beginning with the second paragraph, state the supporting details to justify your purpose. These may take the form of background information, statistics or first-hand accounts. A few short paragraphs within the body of the letter should be enough to support your reasoning.

Finally, in the closing paragraph, briefly restate your purpose and why it is important. If the purpose of your letter is employment related, consider ending your letter with your contact information. However, if the purpose is informational, think about closing with gratitude for the reader's time.

After writing the body of the letter, type the closing, followed by a comma, leave 3 blank lines, then type your name and title (if applicable), all flush left. Sign the letter in the blank space above your typed name. Now doesn't that look professional?

Sincerely,

John Doe

Administrative Assistant

Modified Block Format

January 16, 2007

5 Hill Street

Madison, Wisconsin 53700

Ms. Helen Jones

President

Jones, Jones & Jones

23 International Lane

Boston, Massachusetts 01234

Dear Ms. Jones:

The first paragraph of a typical business letter is used to state the main point of the letter. Begin with a friendly opening; then quickly transition into the purpose of your letter. Use a couple of sentences to explain the purpose, but do not go in to detail until the next paragraph.

Beginning with the second paragraph, state the supporting details to justify your purpose. These may take the form of background information, statistics or first-hand accounts. A few short paragraphs within the body of the letter should be enough to support your reasoning.

Finally, in the closing paragraph, briefly restate your purpose and why it is important. If the purpose of your letter is employment related, consider ending your letter with your contact information. However, if the purpose is informational, think about closing with gratitude for the reader's time.

After writing the body of the letter, type the closing, followed by a comma, leave 3 blank lines, then type your name and title (if applicable), all flush left. Sign the letter in the blank space above your typed name. Now doesn't that look professional?

Sincerely,

John Doe

Administrative Assistant

Semi-block format

January 16, 2007

5 Hill Street

Madison, Wisconsin 53700

Ms. Helen Jones

President

Jones, Jones & Jones

23 International Lane

Boston, Massachusetts 01234

Dear Ms. Jones:

The first paragraph of a typical business letter is used to state the main point of the letter. Begin with a friendly opening; then quickly transition into the purpose of your letter. Use a couple of sentences to explain the purpose, but do not go in to detail until the next paragraph.

Beginning with the second paragraph, state the supporting details to justify your purpose. These may take the form of background information, statistics or first-hand accounts. A few short paragraphs within the body of the letter should be enough to support your reasoning.

Finally, in the closing paragraph, briefly restate your purpose and why it is important. If the purpose of your letter is employment related, consider ending your letter with your contact information. However, if the purpose is informational, think about closing with gratitude for the reader's time.

After writing the body of the letter, type the closing, followed by a comma, leave 3 blank lines, then type your name and title (if applicable), all flush left. Sign the letter in the blank space above your typed name. Now doesn't that look professional?

Sincerely,

John Doe

Administrative Assistant

Organize Your Writing - Memo Writing

A memo is a means of transmitting official and professional information or a message to persons in the office or organization. Memos are informative or persuasive, and may serve their simple purposes, more complex memos are often needed in an office setting Memos solve problems either by informing the reader about new information, like policy changes, price increases, etc., or by persuading the reader to take an action, such as attend a meeting, use less paper, or change a current production procedure. Regardless of the specific goal, memos are most effective when they connect the purpose of the writer with the interests and needs of the reader.

Basic Memo Plans

Standard office memos can be approached in different ways to fit your purpose. Here are three basic plans:

The direct plan, which is the most common, starts out by stating the most important points first and then moves to supporting details. This plan is useful for routine information and for relaying news.

The indirect plan makes an appeal or spews out evidence first and arrives at a conclusion based on these facts. This plan is best used when you need to arouse your reader's interest before describing some action that you want taken.

A combination approach can be used for the balanced plan. This plan is particularly useful when relaying bad news, as it combines information and persuasion

Parts of a Memo

Standard memos are divided into segments to organize the information and to help achieve the writer's purpose.

Heading Segment

The heading segment follows this general format:

TO : (readers' names and job titles)

FROM : (your name and job title)

DATE : (complete and current date)

SUBJECT : (what the memo is about, highlighted in some way)

Make sure you address the reader by his or her correct name and job title.

Be specific and concise in your subject line.

Opening : The purpose of a memo is usually found in the opening paragraphs and is presented in three parts: the context and problem, the specific assignment or task, and the purpose of the memo.

The context is the event, circumstance, or background of the problem you are solving. You may use a paragraph to establish the background and state the problem or simply the opening of a sentence, Include only what your reader needs, but be sure it is clear.

In the task statement you should describe what you are doing to help solve the problem. If the action was requested, your task may be indicated by a sentence opening like,

Finally, the purpose statement of a memo gives your reason for writing it and forecasts what is in the rest of the memo. This is not the time to be shy. You want to come right out and tell your reader the kind of information that's in store.

Summary : If your memo is longer than a page, you may want to include a separate summary segment. This segment provides a brief statement of the key recommendations you have reached. These will help your reader understand the key points of the memo immediately. This segment may also include references to methods and sources you have used in your research, but remember to keep it brief.

Discussion : The discussion segments are the parts in which you get to include all the juicy details that support your ideas. Keep these two things in mind:

Begin with the information that is most important. This may mean that you will start with key findings or recommendations. Start with your most general information and move to your specific or supporting facts. For easy reading, put important points or details into lists rather than paragraphs when possible. Be careful to make lists parallel in grammatical form. **(Stay away from jargon your reader may not understand. If your work is** very technical, but the person you are writing to is not well versed in that field, stick to words that person will understand)

Conclusion : Now you're almost done. After the reader has absorbed all of your information, you want to close with a courteous ending that states what action you want your reader to take. Make sure you consider how the reader will benefit from the desired actions and how you can make those actions easier.

Format of Memo

Semantics Space
(Inter Office Memorandum)

TO : Office secretaries and Superintendents
From : The Chief Purchase Officer

Subject : Indent for the requirement of chairs

As discussed in the Executive board meeting held on Jan 4,2007, an order has been placed for the supply of 200 office chairs with Bantia Furniture Mart and they shall be delivering us the chairs on Jan 20,2007 . Please send the indent for the chairs you require before Jan 15,2007.

CC: General Manager   **Hari Rao**

Effective Email - How to communicate powerfully by email

"The phonomenal growth in the use of the internet has resulted in services that millions of people now take for granted, such as e-mail, web browsing and electronic exchange of business transactions"-

Geird kesser

Employers look for potential employees with effective communication skills. The job search process is documentation of both your written and oral skills. Your written communication should clearly enunciate your competencies and positively represent you to the employer. An effective letter demonstrates your professional communication skills, competencies relevant to an open or potential position, enthusiasm and motivation for a specific position or type of work, and your research about the employer.

Are you aware that one of the most time-consuming, yet important tasks busy employees have on their to-do lists is writing? E-mail inboxes are full of messages requiring responses to be sent out to those with equally overflowing message centers. The quantity of time spent to write letters, memos, proposals, and technical reports often exceeds the quality of the resulting documents.

Electronic mail (email) may be a "last chance" medium for developing the writing skills of students and employees. Students, and just about everyone else, are now addicted to the electronic medium, and there is no turning back. My purpose here is not to repeat easily found information with a few keywords on the Internet, but to ask the reader to reflect more comprehensively on the nature of the changing communication medium and the positive effects these changes may have on improving students' and workers' writing skills.

Employees find it difficult to rely on traditional form letters when writing email, making email a creative writing activity. Email requires writing — lots of writing — sorting, categorizing, deleting, typing, and evaluating. If nothing else, email reveals the problems the writer has with grammar, thought construction, paragraph development, style, and other matters related to cognition. email has its own "language" made up of icons, abbreviations, acronyms, emoticons, and other examples of metaphorical writing. Email seems to lie somewhere between written communication and oral communication.

Email Etiquette

Since email is part of the virtual world of communication, many people communicate in their email messages the same way they do in virtual chat rooms: with much less formality and sometimes too aggressively. Email etiquette offers some guidelines that all writers can use to facilitate better communication between themselves and their readers.

- Electronic mail is the medium of communication that sends and receives messages through specially designed computer networks.
- E-Mails are quick transmission of information and ideas

One overall point to remember is that an email message does not have non-verbal expression to supplement what we are "saying." Most of the time we make judgments about a person's motives and intentions based on their tone of voice, gestures, and their proximity to us. When those are absent it becomes more difficult to figure out what the message sender means. It is much easier to offend or hurt someone in email and that is why it is important to be as clear and concise as possible

There are a few simple rules to ensure that your emails are read in the first place and stay useful to the recipient

- **Be concise and to the point :** Remember that reading an email is harder than reading printed communications.
- **Answer all questions, and pre-empt further questions.**
- **Use proper spelling, grammar and punctuation:** Improper spelling, grammar and punctuation give a bad impression of your company.
- **Make it personal.**
- **Use templates for frequently used responses.**
- **Answer swiftly:** Each email should be replied to within at least 24 hours, and preferably within the same working day.
- **Do not attach unnecessary files.**
- **Use proper structure and layout:** Use short paragraphs and blank lines between each paragraph.
- **Do not overuse the High Priority option.**
- **Do not write in CAPITALS:** IF YOU WRITE IN CAPITALS, IT SEEMS AS IF YOU ARE SHOUTING.
- **Don't leave out the message thread:** In other words, click "Reply" instead of "New Mail."

- **Add disclaimers to your emails.**
- **Read the email before you send it:** Reading your email through the eyes of the recipient will help you send a more effective message and avoid misunderstandings and inappropriate comments.
- **Do not overuse "Reply to All."**
- **Take care with abbreviations and emoticons:** The recipient might not be aware of the meanings of the abbreviations, and in business emails these are generally not appropriate. If you are not sure whether your recipient knows what an emoticon means, don't use it.
- **Be careful with formatting.**
- **Take care with rich text and HTML messages:** Be aware that when you send an email in Rich Text or HTML format, the sender might be able to receive only plain text emails.
- **Do not forward chain letters.**
- **Do not request delivery and read receipts.**
- **Do not ask to recall a message.**
- **Do not copy a message or attachment without permission:** If you do not ask permission first, you might be infringing on copyright laws.
- **Do not use email to discuss confidential information.**
- **Use a meaningful subject.**
- **Use active instead of passive voice:** "We will process your order today" sounds better than "Your order will be processed today."
- **Avoid using URGENT and IMPORTANT.**
- **Avoid long sentences:** Try to keep your sentences to a maximum of 15-20 words. Email is meant to be a quick medium and requires a different kind of writing than letters.
- **Don't send or forward emails containing libelous, defamatory, offensive, racist or obscene remarks.**
- **Don't forward virus hoaxes.**
- **Keep your language gender neutral:** Avoid using sexist language such as "The user should add a signature by configuring his email program."
- **Don't reply to spam.**

Advantages of e-mail.

- *Speed*
- *Low Cost*
- *Quick Distribution*
- *Flexibility*
- *Easy Attachments*
- *Easy up-ward Communications*

Characteristics of Successful e-mail Messages

- *Concise*
- *Correct*
- *Clear*
- *Conversational Tone*
- *Single Theme*

General Format : The Basics

- Write a salutation for each new subject email.
- Try to keep the email brief (one screen length).
- Return emails within the same time you would a phone call.
- Check for punctuation, spelling, and grammatical errors
- Use caps when appropriate.
- Format your email for plain text rather than HTML.
- Use a font that has a professional or neutral look.

A Wise Camel

A mother and a baby camel were lazing around, and suddenly the baby camel asked....

Baby : Mother, mother, may I ask you some questions?

Mother : Sure! Why son, is there something bothering you?

Baby: Why do camels have humps?

Mother : Well son, we are desert animals, we need the humps to store water and we are known to survive without water

Baby : Okay, then why are our legs long and our feet rounded?

Mother : Son, obviously they are meant for walking in the desert, You know with these legs I can move around the desert better than anyone does! Said the mother proudly.

Baby : Okay, then why are our eyelashes long? Sometimes it bothers my sight.

Mother : My son, those long thick eyelashes are your protective cover. They help to protect your eyes from the desert sand and wind. Said mother camel with eyes rimming with pride....

Baby : I see. So the hump is to store water when we are in the desert, the legs are for walking through the desert and these eyelashes protect my eyes from the desert...

Then what the hell are we doing here in the Zzzoooooo!

Moral of the Story Is :

"Skills, knowledge, abilities and experiences are only useful if you are at the right place

""Quote of the day: Love your job but never fall in love with your company, because you never know when the company stops loving you!!""

A Letter
From Abraham Lincoln to his son's teacher

He will have to learn, I know, that all men are not just, all men are not true.

But teach him also that for every scoundrel, there is a hero; that for every selfish politician, there is a dedicated leader. Teach him, that for every enemy, there is a friend. It will take time, I know but teach him if you can, that a dollar earned is of far more value than five found.

Teach him to learn to lose and also to enjoy winning. Steer him away from envy if you can, teach him the secret of quite laughter .Let him learn early that the bullies are the easiest to lick.

Teach him if you can the wonders of books, but also give him quite time to ponder the eternal mystery of birds in the sky, bees in the sun and flowers on a green hill side.

In school teach him it is far more honorable to fail than to cheat. Teach him to have faith in his own ideas, even if every one tells him they are wrong. Teach him to be gentle with gentle people and tough with the tough.

Try to give my son the strength not to follow the crowd when everyone is getting on the bandwagon. Teach him to listen to all men but teach him also to filter all he hears on a screen of truth, and take only the good that comes through.

Teach him if you can, how to laugh if he is sad. Teach him there is no shame in tears. Teach him there to scoff at cynics and to beware of too much sweetness. Teach him to sell his brawn and brain to the highest bidders but never to put a price-tag on his heart and soul. Teach him to close his ears to a howling mob and to stand and fight if he thinks he is right.

Treat him gently, but do not cuddle him, because only the test of fire makes fine steel. Let him have the courage to be impatient, let him have the patience to be brave. Teach him always to have a sublime faith in himself, because then he will always have sublime faith in mankind. This is a big order, but see what you can do.

He is such a fine little fellow, my son!!!!!!

BIBLIOGRAPHY

Adler A. Communication at work. London, McGraw-Hill, 1993

Alec Fisher, Critical thinking, Pub. Cambridge University Press

Arons.Y.Paula Reading skills

Arthur D. Rosenberg, David V. Hizer, The Resume Handbook: How to Write Outstanding Resumes & Cover Letters for Every Situation (ResumeHandbook),

Article Career development and job-search advice for new college graduates

Article,Dated January 17, 2007 The Hindu

Baland, B 7Clanchy,J Study Abroad,Longman, Australia,1984

Becham Clive and Hartley Peter, Business communication , Business & Economic ,2002

Bone D. A Practical Guide to Effective Listening. London, Kogan Page, 1988

Burdess, N The handbook on students skills, Illustrations from Burdes Prentice Hall, Victoria 1991

Business Communication, by Harvard Business School Press,2005.

David James & Anthony Masters , Letter Writing Skills 3Rev Ed edition (1 Jan 2003)

Donald R. Clark, Big Dog little dog, 1998.

DukerS. Listening: Reading. Vol.II. Scarecrow Press,1971

Eisenberg A. Effective Technical Communication (McGraw-Hill 1992).

Frank S. Endicott., Adapted From The Endicott Report: Trends in Employment of College and University Graduates in Business and Industry (29th Annual Report).

Gerard M Blair, Presentation Skills for Emergent Managers.

Guffey Ellen Mary, Business Communication, 3rd edition 2002,Thomson-South western.

Howard 2002, Lauckner 2002, McGinnis 2001.

Ian Mackay, Listening Skills, Second edition,University Press (India) Ltd.

Jan Perrett, Job Hunting after University or College Pub. Kogan Page.

Janis Grummit, A Guide to Interviewing Skills, The Industrial Society, 1980

Kathryn K. Troutman, Ten Steps to a Federal Job.

Kelly, M. & Stafford, K., Managing Small Group Discussion, Professional Development Unit, City University of Hong Kong, 1993, pp.8-11.

Konradt., "How To Improve Your Lousy Writing Skills In The Workplace

Michael Purdy, Listening in Everyday Life.

Murphy, J. M. 1991. Oral communication in TESOL: Integrating speaking, listening and pronunciation. TESOL Quarterly, 25.

NACE's 2003 Planning Job Choices,NewsDay Article.

Nancy Halligan, Technical Writing2001

Nicholas Lore, THE PATHFINDER: How To Choose or Change Your Career for a Lifetime of Satisfaction and Success, 2003.

Perry Anne Leslie,Woodington Coleman Cynthia. Teaching Basic Skills,1985

Picardi Richard, Skills of workplace communication,, 2001.

Prasad B, Kataria and Sons, Applied Indian communication Techniques,

Randall S. Hansen, Ph.D. and Katharine Hansen, The Importance of Good Writing Skills, 1996.

Robert W. Bly, Improving Your Listening Skills.

Steven C. Martin & Catherine A. Martin, Talk to Me: How to Create Positive, Loving Communication.", 1996

Suzette Haden Elgin, "Staying Well With The Gentle Art of Verbal Self-Defense,

Tom Antion's new book, Wake em Up: How to Use Humor and Other Professional Techniques to Create Alarmingly Good Business Presentations. Anchor Publishing

Turk Christofer, Effective writing- Improving Scientific, Technical Business communication,1989

Van Emden J. and Easteal J. Technical Writing and Speaking, an Introduction (McGraw-Hill 1996

Wajnryb, R. 1991. "Active listening": An effective strategy in language learning. English Teaching Forum, 29, 1, pp. 30-31.

Wallace, M Study skills in English 1980

Winckel, A. & Hart, B. Report writing style guide for engineering students. 3 rd. edn, 1996.

Yana parker, The Damn Good Resume Guide,

Websites

http://www.ucc.ie/careers/
www.teachingenglish.org.uk
htpp://www.libraries.mit.edu
http://encarta.msn.com/encnet/features/dictionary/dictionaryhome.aspx
http://www.cde.ca.gov/fg/fo/we/
http://www.technical-writing-course.com/
http://www.techpubs.com/resources.html

Job website

www.yuvajobs.com
www.domnico.com
www.discussionsworld.com
www.koolkampus.com
www.chetanas.com
www.fresherjobs.in
www.rameshkumar.net

www.sansite.info
www.domnico.com
www.timesjob.com
www.maukri.com
www.monster.com
www.careermirchi.com

Company Question paper sites

www.freshersworld.com
www.yuvajobs.com - contains recent papers.
www.dominco.comordominico.com
www.discussionsworld.com
www.koolkampus.com
www.chetanas.com - contains very recent papers. - The most useful group.
www.ittestpapers.com
www.aucse.com
www.vyomworld.com
www.papers4placernent.com
www.placementpapers.com
www.brainvista.com - puzzles
www.exforsys.com - question bank.- range have to check out. www.ascenteducation.com - (aptitude –topic wise like trains, time, etc., available - very useful - created for CAT people)

Milton Keynes UK
Ingram Content Group UK Ltd.
UKHW022129051023
430028UK00005B/170